D0240455

Robinsons

Greenhouse Gardening

the practical guide to success

Robinsons

Greenhouse Gardening

the practical guide to success

Bernard Salt

foreword by Anne Swithinbank

MPC

Published by:
Moorland Publishing Co Ltd,
Moor Farm Road West, Ashbourne, Derbyshire DE6 1HD, England

ISBN 0 86190 506 7

MPC Production:
Editorial & design: John Robey

British Library Cataloguing in Publication Data:
A catalogue record for this book is available from the British Library.

Frontispiece: Robinsons 'Royale' greenhouse

Illustrations have been supplied as follows: Defenders Ltd Fig 120; Diplex Ltd Figs 6, 7; Garden Answers Magazine Fig 87; Garden Direct Fig 37; Holt Studios International Figs 95, 114, 115, 119, 122, 123; Horticulure Research International Fig 118; Multigro Fig 24; Robinsons of Winchester Ltd pages 2, 6; Simply Controls Fig 77; Thermoforce Ltd Figs 12, 19, 35, 44. All other illustrations are by the author.
The author and publisher would like to acknowledge the assistance given by Garden Answers Magazine in obtaining illustrations

Colour origination by: J. Film Process Ltd

Printed in Hong Kong by: Wing King Tong Co Ltd

Contents

The Popular range makes an excellent first greenhouse

Foreword

Owning a greenhouse is the dream of most gardeners. The extra protection offered to plants will open up a whole new world of possibilities, including somewhere to potter on rainy days. I can still remember the magic of owning my first greenhouse. Even though I had to share it with my father's tomatoes and cucumbers, I spent hours inside tending and propagating my plants. With good planning the greenhouse will soon become the nucleus of the garden — protecting tender perennials from winter cold, raising young plants and providing the best environment for crops like tomatoes, aubergines and peppers. A knowledge of propagation soon becomes indispensable, not least to enjoy plant swopping with like-minded friends.

Before the luxury of standing in the doorway of your new greenhouse, a lot of thought and decision-making has to take place. Not least of these is the choice of site, balancing the need for light and wind protection against how the structure will fit into your garden. The novice greenhouse gardener will need to read up on basic necessities and good practices in order to provide adequately for their plants. Early contemplation of staging, shelving, method of heating, shading and insulation will also give a good idea of total cost.

Plants in the greenhouse will be more dependant on their owner than those growing in the soil of beds and borders outside. Suddenly a greater understanding of watering, feeding and pest control is needed. The environment inside a greenhouse is prone to sudden change, so knowing how to avoid dramatic variations in temperature, raise humidity in summer and prevent cold, dank conditions during winter is vital to plant health.

A good morning routine is important, and makes a satisfying start to the day. Open the doors and enjoy the unique smell of warm earth and plants. Check for pests, remove dead leaves, withering flowers and water those plants that need it. Check the atmosphere and adjust equipment as necessary to provide the right conditions for the day ahead. After a while, caring for plants becomes almost instinctive, but only after basic rules have been grasped.

In *Robinsons Greenhouse Gardening*, Bernard Salt presents a no-nonsense practical guide. Unclouded by flights of fantasy, he spells out all the basic procedures necessary to start the greenhouse gardener on a course of success. Only when he has imparted the facts and figures behind this vital knowledge does he open the door to some of the exciting prospects ahead.

Anne Swithinbank

Preface

This book is called *Robinsons Greenhouse Gar dening* and I acknowledge the assistance given to me by the respected greenhouse manufacturers, Robinsons of Winchester. Whether you are fortunate enough to own a Robinsons greenhouse, as I do, or have a different make — this book is equally for you. I have not covered the question of choosing a greenhouse model, but do not make the mistake of buying one that is too small: get as wide a greenhouse as you can afford — you can always extend it later.

This book is aimed at all greenhouse gardeners. Those with their first greenhouse will find the methods described lead to successful propagation and growth, while experienced gardeners will get ideas to increase the use they make of their greenhouse and extend the range of plants they grow.

In gardening there are several methods of growing plants — if a method works for you it is right! The methods described here are those which have worked for my students over the last twenty-six years of teaching the art and science (not to mention the joys!) of plant production.

A greenhouse should be in use for 364 days a year (it is empty for autumn cleaning on the other day). It is invaluable in the production of annuals, biennials and perennials for the flower garden, plants for the conservatory and items for the flower arranger. The usual summer crops of tomatoes, peppers, cucumbers, melons and grapes can be followed by autumn chrysanthemums. Hardy and half-hardy vegetable plants are easily produced in abundance and tender perennials are protected throughout the winter.

The book is not intended to be read in one go, but used as a reference book throughout the year. If you are uncertain of a procedure, take this book into the greenhouse and follow the method described. The timing of seed sowing is very difficult to advise upon as weather on these islands is so varied. A week late is usually better than a week early but gardeners are advised to listen to weather forecasts, especially when late spring frosts are likely in their area.

With the odd exception (these are acknowledged) all photographs were taken in an amateur's greenhouse and garden. The greenhouse is a standard Robinsons Rosette, it has a home-made electric propagator and a propane heater, set to keep the greenhouse just frost free. This greenhouse keeps a two acre garden supplied with plants and its costs are covered by plant sales.

I wish you joy of your greenhouse and hope that this book will increase the pleasure you get from it.

Bernard Salt
January 1994

1

Setting Up & Siting a New Greenhouse

Before a new greenhouse can be installed a good deal of consideration needs to be taken over its siting, how it is to be heated and ventilated, how mains services such as water and electricity are to be supplied, what type of staging and shelves to install, and even what type of plant containers to use in the greenhouse.

Siting

In most gardens the site will be a compromise between what is ideal and what is practical.

The following must all be considered:

- ***Light*** — this is of extreme importance especially in the winter and early spring.
- ***Access*** — Easy access from the house to the greenhouse and a good surface on the path will probably lead to better care for the plants.
- ***Aesthetic*** — the greenhouse needs to look right and fit in with the overall garden design.
- ***Trees*** — these should not shade nor overhang the greenhouse, but when far enough away they can be good wind breaks.
- ***Distance from the boundary*** — a clear area of at least one metre around the greenhouse makes good sense and may provide a useful area for standing boxes of plants.
- ***Wind*** — shelter from cold prevailing winds helps to keep the temperature up. A gap between two buildings will sometimes funnel the wind, so such situations should be avoided.
- ***Foundations*** — firm and *level* ground.
- ***Soil*** — good and free draining, but poor soil can be overcome by creating a raised bed.
- ***Frost*** — avoid frost pockets or hollows.

Also services:

- ***Electricity supply*** — an electric propagator is almost essential and a light very useful.
- ***Water supply*** — a tap inside the greenhouse is ideal.
- ***Natural gas*** — currently the cheapest source of heat (with the exception of sunlight).

Light

Light is the source of heat for the greenhouse and the source of energy for plant growth. The greenhouse must be sited where it will receive the maximum amount of light. Shade from trees and buildings should be avoided and the ridge is best in an east-west direction.

The greenhouse with a ridge that runs east-west will have sunshine on its longest side for most of the day. The greenhouse with a ridge that runs north-south will have sunshine on its gable end for most of the day. This makes little difference with a square greenhouse but a big difference with a rectangular greenhouse. Some areas that are sunny in summer may receive little or no sun in winter time when shadows are much longer; winter sunshine is a very important consideration in selecting the site.

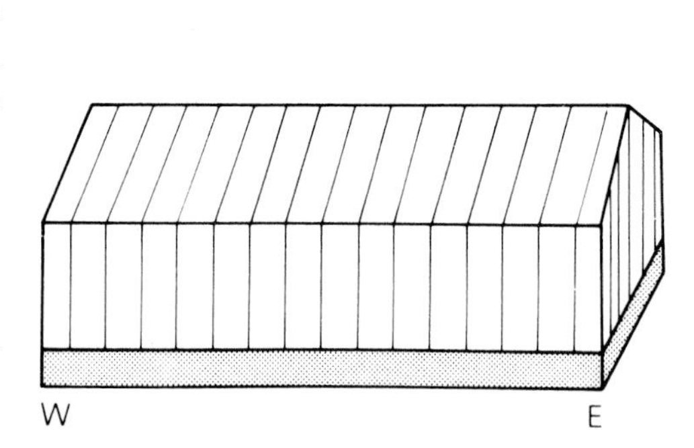

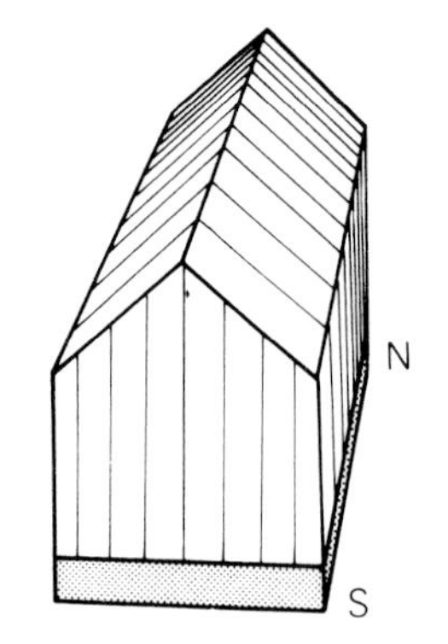

1 The sun's view of two similar-sized greenhouses just after midday. Note the different amount of light that each is getting

Services

Electricity

Electricity can be dangerous and must be installed by a qualified electrician. The whole circuit must be protected with a trip fuse and individual items with a residual current device.

Switches and sockets should be of a waterproof type or housed in a waterproof box as shown in the photograph.

2 Electrical fittings in a waterproof box

Water supply

Water is best laid to the greenhouse before the site is prepared. The pipe needs to be 60cm (2 feet) deep to protect it from frost. A bib tap with a back plate for fixing is a useful type as it has a screw thread to which a hose is easily fitted. The tap however must be fitted with a non-return valve. The majority of greenhouse owners use a hosepipe for a water supply, with a fitting which controls the flow from the users' end.

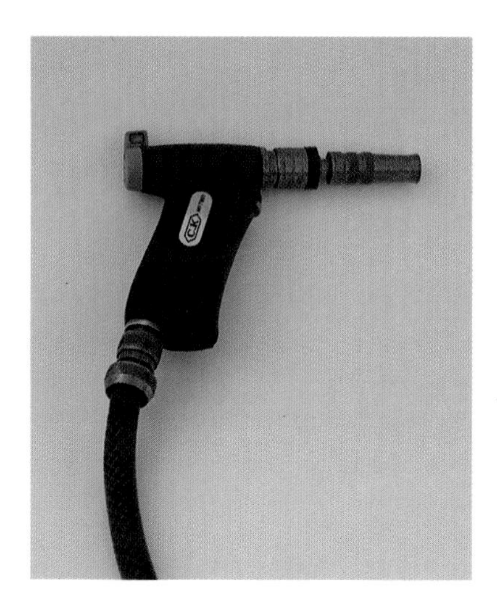

3 This fitting gives the user full control over the flow of water from a hose

Natural Gas

If it is intended to use a gas heater, natural gas should be laid underground by a qualified fitter before the greenhouse is erected. The fumes from burning natural gas will not harm plants.

Foundations

The ground must be levelled and thoroughly compacted, avoid wet hollow places as flooding may undermine the foundations. The Robinsons eaves height of 5ft 6in is 1ft taller than many makes and gives a comfortable working height. (The greenhouse standing on a brick wall, which appears in a number of the photographs in this book, is owned by an exceptionally tall gardener!)

Staging, Benching & Shelving

Benching and staging are very similar, the main difference is that benches have solid tops and staging has a slatted top. A slatted top allows better air flow around the plants, this helps control fungus diseases in autumn, but in summer it makes plants dry out more quickly.

Benches and staging have several purposes:

- Small plants have better light.
- Pots and boxes are at a convenient height for observation, watering etc.
- There is a working area for sowing, potting, taking cuttings, etc.
- Space underneath is useful for the *temporary* storage of composts, pots and trays.
- Where theglass goes almost to the floor (as in a Robinsons greenhouse) the area underneath is a good place to grow chrysanthemum stools, dahlia tubers for cuttings, ferns and other shade tolerant plants.
- Height-adjustable staging is a real boon to back sufferers.
- Benches, shelves and staging help to organise the greenhouse into convenient production unit.

Removable staging, or staging which folds down, allows dual use of a single area. An average handy person could produce home-made benches from a variety of materials; care should be taken however not to provide nooks and crannies which may encourage pests and diseases. Built-in benches are often cheaper and more stable, than free-standing ones. Wooden benches are better when covered with a sheet of white plastic. This is easy to clean, reflects light and looks good. All benches and staging should be level, this is very important for a capillary bed or it will not function properly.

There is a wide range of staging and benches available for purchase, the quality of which is reflected in the price.

The diagram shows the Robinsons two-tier free standing bench. This is supplied in kit form and is available in three lengths: 12in, 22in and 34in, combinations of which can give many different lengths. The overall height is 32in.

Robinsons slatted staging is available in three widths: 18in, 25in and 37in. The 37in is only

4 Robinsons two-tier benching in hygenic, maintenance-free aluminium

5 Robinsons slatted staging and shelving

suitable for the 'Professional' range of greenhouses. The absence of front supports makes this ideal for wheelchair gardeners.

Shelves are extremely useful in a greenhouse, specially when space becomes short in late spring. Plants which sit on shelves have very good light levels and this usually gives better growth.

Robinsons shelving is available in three widths (8in, 12in and 15in) and is obtainable in several lengths. These shelf brackets are fitted to greenhouse glazing bars using special cropped headed bolts for aluminium greenhouses and will support the weight of an eight-stone person. Care should be taken that the cropped headed bolts are in the correct position before they are tightened.

The author (who does not work for Robinsons) finds these shelves to be really excellent and a most valuable addition to his greenhouse.

Heating

A greenhouse is a sun trap — it warms more quickly and cools more slowly than the outside, in addition there is no chill factor from the wind. Large changes in temperature are bad for plants so very high daytime temperatures and very low night-time temperatures must be avoided.

A greenhouse with a lot of material inside will warm up and cool down more slowly than an empty greenhouse. As water holds more heat than any other substance, sealed plastic containers full of water underneath the staging aid the thermal efficiency of the greenhouse. Half a ton of water (500 litres) makes a measurable difference in a 10ft x 8ft greenhouse.

The highest and lowest temperature during a twenty four hour period is easily recorded by use of a maximum and minimum thermometer. One of these is an essential tool in the greenhouse.

All thermometers **must be shaded from direct sunlight** and they should be positioned well away from the glass or the recorded temperatures will be several degrees too high or too low. The best site for a thermometer is just above the plants.

6 (left) A maximum and minimum thermometer. The ***bottom*** *of the riders indicate the highest and lowest temperatures reached since the instrument was last set*

Prevention of Over Heating

At the height of summer a greenhouse can become so warm that some plants are damaged. This is prevented by using the maximum available ventilation (including the door), increasing the humidity by wetting the floor and

7 (right) Electronic thermometers should be protected from splashing water

excluding some of the light by shading. The cheapest form of shading is a mixture of lime and water, sprayed or painted on the outside of the glass; this is also easily removed. Paint-on shadings can be purchased and although these are more expensive they are less likely to be washed off by rain. 'Vari-shade' is a greenhouse shading which becomes transparent when wet and shades when dry, these changes repeating all summer.

It is not necessary to cover the whole of the greenhouse with shading, shade just the south and west facing sides, or the part which will protect the most vunerable plants (these include leafy cuttings, young seedlings, ferns, ivies, African violet, Gloxinia, etc.) Internal blinds are better as they can be raised or lowered according to need. These are available in woven fabrics, plastic meshes and coloured sheets. Internal blinds however can be troublesome, for example they restrict the use of roof glazing bars for plant support. External blinds would be very much better, but the author is not aware of any good external blinds currently available in the UK. Many grades of shade netting are available which can be used externally and are available from good garden centres.

Prevention of Sub-Zero Temperatures in Winter

During a very cold spell, when temperatures remain below freezing both day and night, it is virtually impossible to prevent frost inside a greenhouse without some form of heating.

If you have no heating it may be possible to protect plants from night frost by covering the staging with a 5cm (2in) thick expanded polystyrene board (available from builders' suppliers), stand the plants on this and cover with

Keeping the Cost of Heating to a Minimum

- Make sure that the glass is clean and there are no slipped or broken panes.
- Fill any gap along the eaves with polystyrene or outdoor adhesive tape. There is no need to do this with a Robinsons greenhouse as the glass fits snugly into an aluminium cill.
- Check the door and if necessary fit draught excluder.
- Completely line the greenhouse with bubble plastic. Use the 6mm thick plastic with large bubbles, this is a much better insulator than the 2mm thick plastic with small bubbles, it is also more transparent.

  Take care not to purchase the single wall bubble plastic as this is a packaging material and is not a good insulator.
- Keep tender plants in a propagator.
- Divide the greenhouse in half with bubble plastic sheets and heat just one half, or if you have a Robinsons Professional, purchase a custom-made partition complete with a sliding door.
- Make sure that the heater is fitted with a thermostat and the setting is not too high.
- Do not open the door except when absolutely necessary.

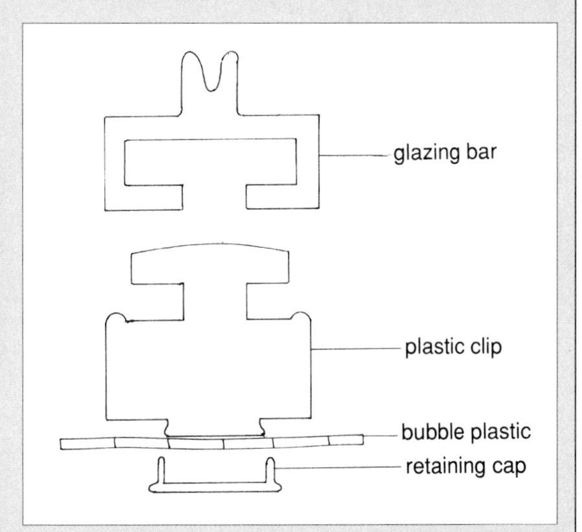

8 This plastic clip fits into the glazing bar channel and holds the bubble plastic at the correct distance from the glass

fleece. At night add an additional cover of aluminium foil — a survival blanket is ideal.

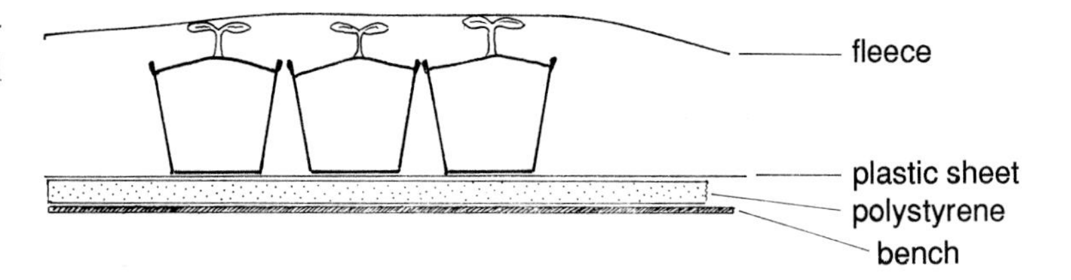

9 Section through an insulated bench

Heaters

The output of a heater is measured in watts (W) or kilowatts (kW). A single bar electric fire produces around 1,000W which is one kilowatt. It is possible that the output of a heater may be still given in the old units — British thermal units (Btu). To convert a Btu figure to kilowatts divide it by 3.4. Example: 10,200Btu divide by 3.4 = 3,000W which is 3kW.

The size of heater required depends upon:

- The size of greenhouse or the size of the heated area inside.
- Whether or not the greenhouse is insulated.
- Which part of the country you live in.
- The minimum temperature required.

The chart below is a guide for the size of heater needed for: A — an insulated greenhouse size 2.4m x 1.8m (8ft x 6ft); and B — an insulated greenhouse size 2.4m x 3m (8ft x 10ft)

It is based on average winter temperatures and assumes that a thermostat is fitted. Note that as there are large local variations in climate in Britain, especially in Scotland, the figures in the table are for guidance only. If a thermostat is fitted to the heater it will only switch on when the temperature falls below the required level. In a greenhouse intended to be kept only frost-free (2 °C/35°F) there will be many nights when the heater does not switch on.

Greenhouse Heater Size

Minimum Temp Required	*2°C (35°F)*		*7°C (45°F)*		*13°C (55°F)*	
Area	*A*	*B*	*A*	*B*	*A*	*B*
South Coast Welsh Coast South West	1kW	1.5kW	2kW	3kW	3kW	3.5kW
London & Home Counties Lancashire Northern Ireland (coast)	1.5kW	2kW	2kW	3kW	3kW	4kW
East Wales	1kW	2kW	2kW	3kW	3kW	4kW
East Anglia Northern Ireland (central) Yorkshire Scottish Lowlands	1.5kW	2kW	2.5kW	3.5kW	3kW	4.5kW
Midlands	1.5kW	2kW	2kW	3.5kW	3kW	5kW
Central Wales Scottish Highlands	1.5kW	2.5kW	2kW	3.5kW	3.5kW	5kW

Choosing a Heater

After deciding on the amount of heat required, the next step is to choose a heater. A wide range of efficient heaters is available for the four main fuels, electricity, paraffin, propane (red bottles) and natural gas. (Butane, usually packed in blue bottles, is unsuitable for use in the greenhouse as its fumes are toxic to plants). All gas heaters discharge water vapour into the air and will therefore increase the humidity, this may be an important consideration, especially in a frost-free greenhouse. Paraffin heaters discharge 14lb of water vapour for each 1lb of paraffin burned; this is rather less than that produced by gas heaters.

The carbon dioxide produced by gas and paraffin heaters is not beneficial to plants as it is produced during cold periods when growth is minimal

If the greenhouse is very near to the house, it may be possible to extend the domestic heating system into it. However as most central heating systems shut down at night, isolating solenoid valves would have to be fitted, together with additional thermostatic controls. This is a job that should be entrusted to a qualified heating engineer.

10 Propane bottles fitted with an automatic change-over valve

Greenhouse Heaters — a Summary

Fuel	*Initial Costs*	*Running Costs*	*Temperature Distribution*	*Notes*
Electricity				
Tube	High	High	Even	Economy night rate reduces cost.
Fan	Average	High	Uneven	Simple to install, accurate control, rapid response. Place near to the door pointing into the greenhouse.
Paraffin	Low	Low	Uneven	Use a premium grade fuel and a 'blue' flame rather than a 'yellow' one. Needs frequent filling. Simple to instal and move. Many without thermostats. Few paraffin heaters give out more than 2kW.
Propane	High	Average	Uneven	Needs two bottles and a change-over valve.
Natural gas	High	Low	Uneven	Rapid response, good thermostatic control.

Ventilating the Greenhouse

Ventilation in a greenhouse has more to do with temperature and humidity control than with supplying air to the plants. Plants in a properly ventilated domestic greenhouse will never be short of either oxygen or carbon dioxide.

Discounting the door, there are two ways of admitting air to a greenhouse: ridge vents and side vents. In still conditions ridge vents allow warm stale air to leave and be replaced by fresh air. Ridge vents provide gentle ventilation and should always be opened first. Side vents give more positive ventilation and are only opened when the ridge vents are fully operative and the house is still too warm. In windy conditions ridge vents provide more positive ventilation as air is admitted by one vent and discharged by another on the opposite side. Ideal ventilation is provided by both top and bottom vents.

An automatic vent controller consists of a cylinder of wax which operates a piston as it expands and contracts. These automatic ventilators are supplied as standard with Robinsons Professional range. For most greenhouses they should be set to begin to open as the temperature approaches 20°C (68°F). This will provide ventilation if the greenhouse is left unattended all day. In very hot weather the door can provide additional ventilation — the double doors of the Royale and Rosette range have a considerable advantage over single doors.

Rapid air movements can cause water stress in plants which will seriously impair their growth. Plants should be arranged so that they are not in a direct draught.

On damp autumn days it is often necessary to ventilate the greenhouse in order to reduce the humidity and control fungus diseases. In these conditions, the automatic vents should be adjusted to open at lower temperatures.

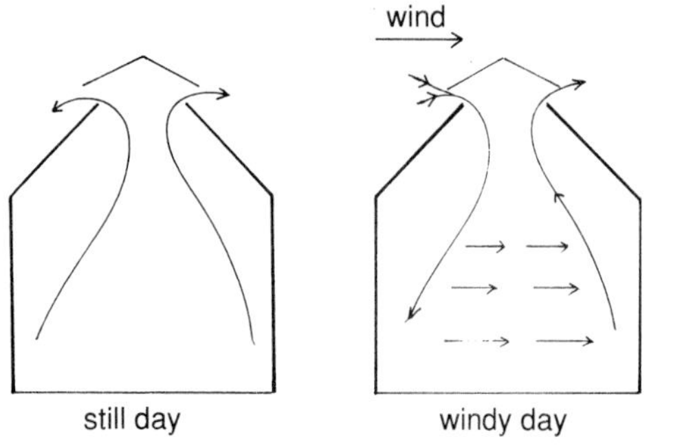

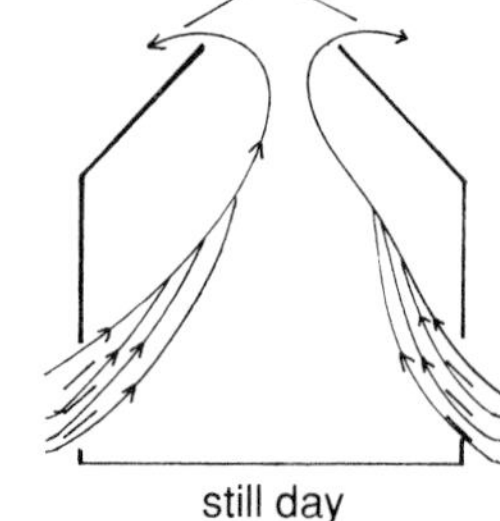

11 Ventilation with top vents only open (left, centre) and both top and bottom vents open (right)

12 Automatic openers on a ridge vent

Soil Warming Cables

A soil warming cable is a complete electric circuit sealed to a three-pin mains plug. A heating element runs along its entire length and connects at the far end to a return wire. The circuit has an earth, in the form of a sheath, and the whole cable is sealed in a waterproof casing. Thermostats for soil warming cables are available and some manufacturers supply cables with thermostats already fitted. It is not possible to reduce, or extend, the length of a soil warming cable; double check the length required before purchasing. **For safety isolate all electrical fittings with a residual current device.**

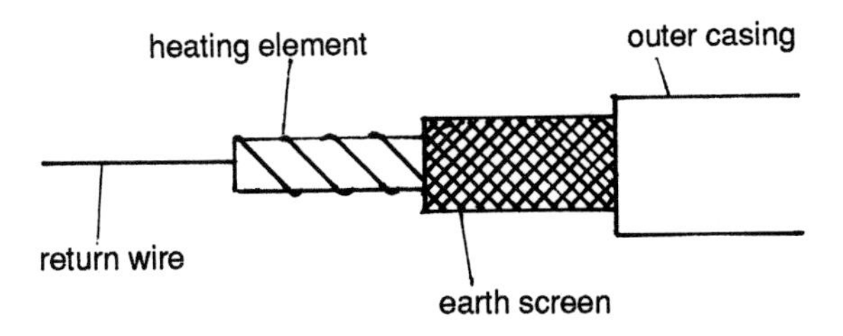

13 *Section through a soil warming cable*

The length of cable varies with the electrical rating, a 75 watt cable will be around 6 metres long and will warm an area of around three quarters of a square metre. The actual area will depend upon the temperature required and whether or not the greenhouse is heated. A soil warming cable is buried 15-20cm (6-8in) below the soil surface in loops 15cm (6in) apart. Care must be taken to keep the pattern regular otherwise uneven heating will result. On no account should the cable cross itself as there may be overheating and cable damage.

The cable is buried in soil or sand. Peat should not be used as it is a bad heat conductor. A cable can be left switched on continuously (preferably with a thermostat) or it may be on a time switch, heating the soil only at night. Running costs can be reduced by using low tariff night-rate electricity.

Uses for soil warming cables:

- ***Early crops*** — Carrots, lettuces, radishes and turnips are all fairly frost hardy and respond well to warm soil. These crops can be produced very early in the year when grown in a warmed bed, especially if they are covered with horticultural fleece. The value of the crop must be considered alongside the cost of the electricity used. This cost is about 0.5 of a unit of electricity per day for each square metre warmed. Electricity cost is reduced by burying a sheet of polystryene (wrapped in plastic sheeting) 5cm (2in) below the cable.

In summer melons show a worthwhile response to warmed soil, but with many crops there is little or no difference at this time of year.

- ***As the Heat Source for a Propagator*** — Soil warming cables are an excellent heat source for a home-made propagator.

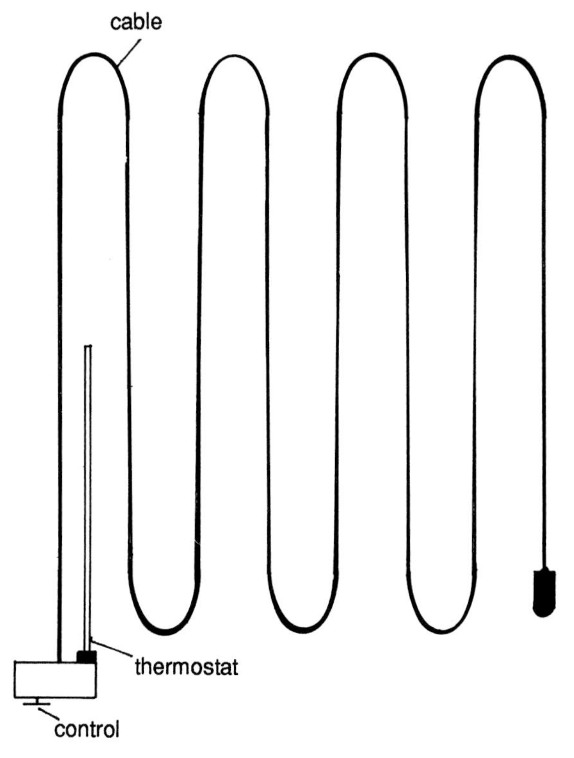

14 *A soil warming cable correctly laid out*

Propagators

In an unheated greenhouse a well used propagator extends the growing season by a full month. It also removes the need to purchase annual crop plants, for example tomatoes and slow growing annual flowers such as lobelia and begonias. Later in the year a propagator can be used to raise more exotic house plants and in winter it protects tender plants.

A propagator consists of a base and a ventilated transparent cover in which plant material is kept in a humid and warm atmosphere. A propagator is easily made by a handy person and there are many different types available for purchase.

Cable Size Needed to Heat a Home-Made Propagator

Propagator Size (square metres)	*Cable Length (metres)*	*Electrical Rating (Watts)*
0.75	6	75
1.5	12	150
3.0	24	300
6.0	48	600

15 This home-made propagator in a Robinsons Royale greenhouse is made from slotted angle (Dexion) and wood. The base is seven-ply marine wood and it holds a 15cm (6in) depth of sand. Heating is by a 75 watt soil warming cable and a rod thermostat is fitted. The front consists of a sheet of bubble plastic that rolls up for access. The propagator is also used as a frost-free area in an otherwise unheated greenhouse, which accounts for it being rather high. A section of sand has been dug up to show the soil warming cable

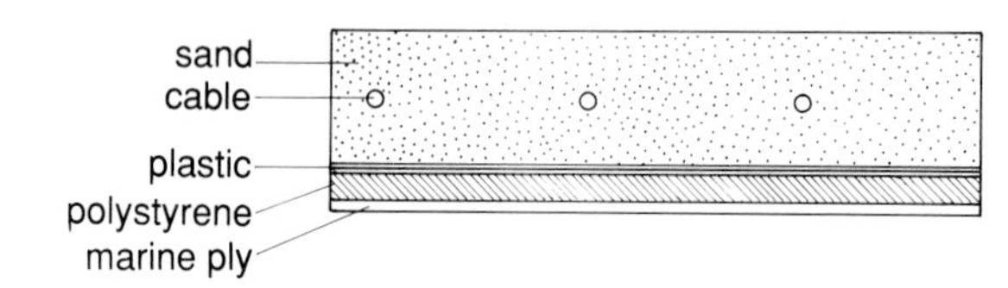

16 Section through the floor of a home-made propagator

17 (right) Section through a propagator

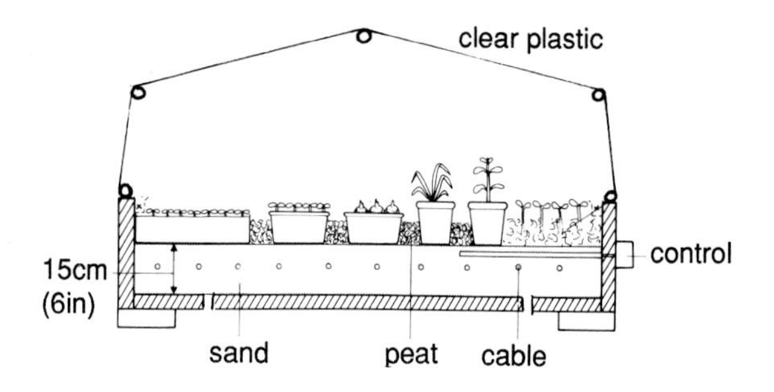

The base of a propagator has drainage holes, moisture being retained by means of capillary matting or a depth of very coarse sand. Some heating is necessary and ideally this is controlled by a thermostat. There must also be some means of shading to prevent overheating by direct sunlight.

Unheated propagators are also available, but apart from their appearance and ease of use, these give no more advantage than a plastic bag.

Propagators without thermostats have low electrical ratings. They may fail to raise the inside temperature high enough to give good germination during cold spells.

Propagator Use

An electrically heated propagator greatly increases the value of a greenhouse. Seeds germinate more quickly and evenly. The success rate with softwood, semi-ripe, bud and leaf cuttings is increased. A well-used propagator extends the growing season by at least four weeks and allows plants to be raised which would otherwise have to be purchased.

With the exception of a greenhouse, a propagator is the best investment a gardener can make.

Properly used a propagator is never empty; there are always seeds to germinate, cuttings to root or tender plants to protect.

18 A large propagator, constructed in aluminium, which holds twelve standard seed trays. The base is insulated with polystyrene and the cover is well ventilated. The heating element is sandwiched between sheets of foil to spread the heat; it is thermostatically controlled and has an electrical rating of 175 Watts.

19 A four-tray capacity propagator, heated by a 75W soil warming cable

Plant Containers

The choice of pots, trays and other containers is very wide and it is important that the best container is used for each situation. If only a few seedlings are required a Continental pot should be used as this will take less space in the propagator than a large seed tray. Small bedding plants like alyssums are fine when grown fifty plants per standard tray, but tomato plants would be almost useless grown in this way and are much better in individual pots.

Square pots take up less bench space than round pots and are the best choice for food plants, whereas house plants are better in round pots as most jardinières take this shape of pot.

Plastic pots have almost completely replaced clay pots as they are more hygenic, lighter and cheaper. Plastic pots have several drainage holes and are ideal for use on a capillary bed. For similar reasons plastic trays have replaced wooden ones.

Note that for some types of plants (eg orchids) clay pots are better than plastic pots as they 'breath' and are easier to water.

Plastic Plant Pots

The size of a pot refers to its internal diameter at the top; the size of large container-type pots usually refers to their volume in litres. Size for size full pots are deeper than Continental, they hold extra compost and are better for mature plants. Continental pots are better for seeds and cuttings as they use less compost. The larger base of the Continental pot makes it more stable and a little better for capillary watering.

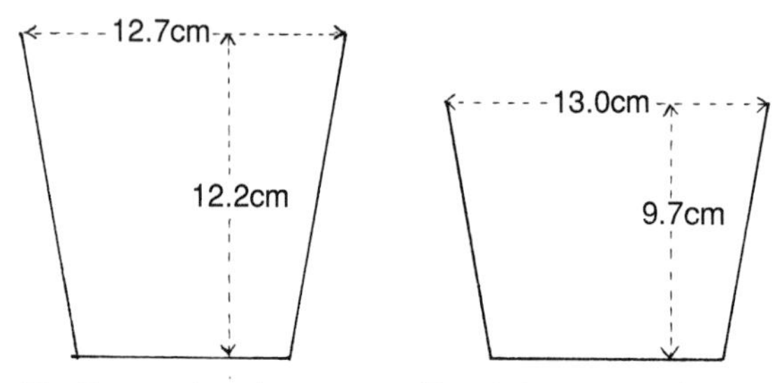

20 Comparison between Full and Continental '5 inch' pots

Polythene Plant Pots

Lay-flat polythene plant pots are used by some commercial growers to cut costs. These are available to the amateur gardener but are not recommended as they are difficult to fill, do not stand well and often need cutting in order to remove the plant.

Peat Pots

Peat pots are made from a mixture of peat and wood. When planting out there is no root disturbance as the pot is planted as well. Peat pots are light and pleasant to handle when dry but are likely to tear when wet. Watering peat pots requires some extra skill and new growers are recommended to try a few in the first instance.

Jiffy-7s

A Jiffy-7 is a compressed peat disc in a fine plastic mesh. When wetted a Jiffy-7 swells to full size in a few minutes. Jiffy-7s are excellent for cuttings and for individual sowing of small seeds. Forty Jiffy-7s just fill a standard seed tray, they are easy to water and are unlikely to become too wet. Jiffy-7s for seed sowing are best expanded by immersion while those for cuttings should be placed in very shallow water or on a capillary mat, this latter method draws extra air into the peat.

A similar product to Jiffy-7 is available in a

21 Jiffy-7s flat and expanded

holder, complete with water tray and transparent cover. These produce excellent results with both seeds and cuttings, but do not leave the cover on too long. Obtainable from: Multigro, 798-800 Pershore Road, Selly Park, Birmingham B29 7NG

Plastic Seed Trays
Plastic seed trays are clean, light and easy to store. They are very good for germinating small seeds and for growing small bedding plants. The disadvantages of trays are that plants in them cannot be given extra space and there is considerable root disturbance when planting out. If a full size tray of moist compost is lifted by one hand it will probably break, two hands should always be used when lifting full trays.

Polystryene Trays with Individual Segments
These are usually sold under the name of Prop-

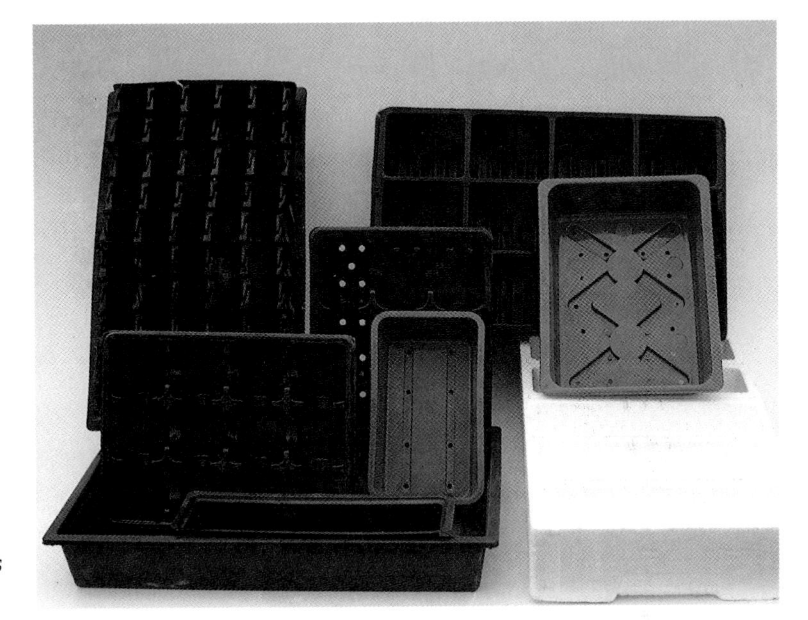

22 *There are many different types of seeds trays available*

23 *(right) Seedlings growing in a divided plastic tray*

24 (above) The 'Multigrow' system

25 (below) Cabbage plants growing in root trainers

a-paks and come as a kit complete with a pusher to eject the plants. They are quick and easy to fill and make good use of bench space. They give good results with small seedlings, especially with early vegetables. Prop-a-paks are bulky and difficult to store, algae tends to grow on the polystryene and is difficult to clean off.

Inserts for Trays

There is a large range of vacuum-formed inserts for seed trays, these are flimsy but effective and with care will last for more than one season. The main advantage of inserts is that planting out is done with the minimum of root disturbance. When using inserts extra care must be taken with watering or the plants in the corner sections remain dry.

Root Trainers

A root trainer consists of a piece of vacuum formed plastic which, when folded in half, forms a number of plant cells. Ten of these are packed into a frame and this holds the cell bases clear of the bench. In the cells the roots are directed downwards by a series of vertical ribs, when the root tip emerges it dehydrates and dies; this encourages the formation of lateral roots in the body of the cell. Plants are released by simply opening the trainer like the page of a book (see Fig 108, page 91). Root trainers are excellent for large seeds like beans, peas and sweet corn; they are also very good for striking cuttings.

Peat Blocks

Peat blocks are made from a special blocking compost which is available from the larger garden centres. The compost is wetted and a special tool presses it into individual cubes.

Several sizes are available, but the 4cm (2in) cube is probably the best, as forty of these pack neatly into a standard seed tray — five rows of eight. One seed is placed in the centre of each block and pressed into it with a cocktail stick.

26 Square pots use all the available space on a bench. As the plants grow the pots must be moved apart to prevent the plants from touching

Pricking out is unnecessary and the resulting plants are transplanted from the trays with minimum root disturbance.

Modules

Trays designed to produce plants with small individual root balls — plant plugs — are being used by commercial growers on a large scale.

Plants can be grown in these module trays by the amateur gardener, but a good deal of skill is required. Better results are obtained if the module tray is placed on a capillary bed (see pages 35-6).

2

Understanding Plants

The purpose of a greenhouse is not just to keep plants warm; it is to create an environment in which plants can thrive. A plants' external environment has six parts: air, light, water, temperature, mineral salts and acidity, all of these can be controlled to some extent by the greenhouse gardener. This chapter gives an outline of these six factors.

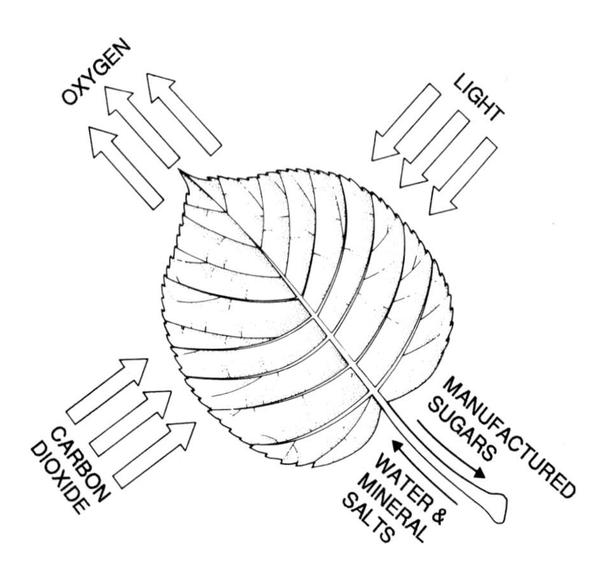

27 *Leaves exchange gases with the atmosphere*

Air

Plants exchange gasses with the atmosphere, when plants are growing their leaves remove carbon dioxide from the air and return oxygen to it. Roots need a constant supply of oxygen, this they obtain from soil air. It is important to have plenty of air spaces in a compost to supply the oxygen that roots need. In waterlogged conditions, roots (and the base of cuttings) cannot get oxygen, they turn black and die.

Seeds cannot germinate without a supply of oxygen. Seed composts therefore must have many air spaces.

Light

Plants use energy to grow, push roots through the soil, pump minerals to their leaves and for many more purposes. Light is the plants' energy supply so without it the plant will die.

Plants use blue and red light and reflect the unwanted green, that is why most plants are green. Surplus energy is stored in sugar and starch.

Daylight varies in two ways — brightness and day-length. The longer the day the more light a plant gets and the more growing time it has. The brighter the light, the faster a plant will

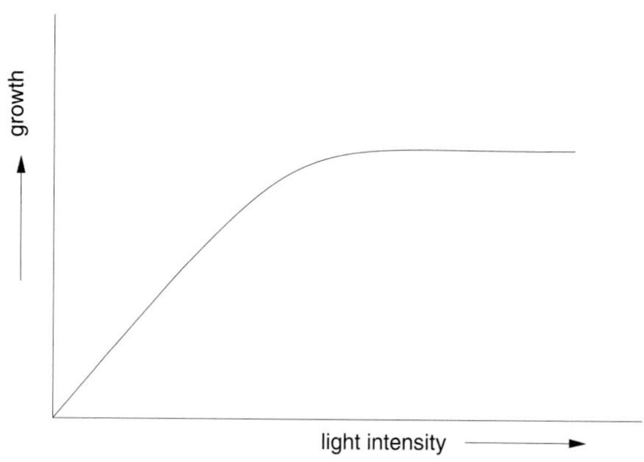

28 *Graph showing the effect of increasing the light intensity on a plant's growth*

grow, there is a limit however and when that is reached extra brightness makes no difference.

During winter, low light levels and short days restrict the growth a plant can make. That is why later sown tomatoes and bedding plants often catch up with those sown too early.

In some species day-length controls flowering time. For instance commercial chrysanthemum growers obtain blooms out of season by shortening the days with black polythene.

Seeds need light to germinate; with some species just a second or two is enough, but others (eg parsley) require very much more.

Water

Plants use water in three ways:

• To transport minerals from the compost to the leaves.

• To keep the leaves turgid (stiff). Water in a plant cell does the same job as air in a tyre.

• They combine water with carbon dioxide to make sugar.

A plant is like a wick, constantly moving water from the compost to the air. Water enters the plant's roots and flows up very fine tubes to the leaves, over 98 per cent of this water evaporates into the air. The rate at which plants lose water depends upon temperature, wind speed and humidity. A higher temperature, a higher windspeed and a lower humidity all increase the rate at which plants lose water. Damping down in hot days or having moist gravel under pot plants are both done to increase humidity and reduce water loss from the leaves.

Seeds also need water to germinate.

Temperature

The temperature of the atmosphere **and** the temperature of the soil or compost is of extreme importance to plant growth and development. The air temperature fluctuates much more than the soil temperature and is usually at a different level. Raising the compost temperature affects the time taken for cuttings to root. It also increases the growth rate of plants.

Cucumber plants will fail if the compost temperature is below 9°C (48°F).

The movement of air affects the temperature. Wind makes the air feel cold — the weather forecasters call this the 'chill factor'. Greenhouse plants are unaffected by wind in this way but lack of wind makes them less robust than outside plants. In Japan many growers stroke their seedlings with a mechanical device to simulate wind. When they are moved outside, 'stroked' plants harden off more quickly than unstroked ones.

Mineral Salts

Sixteen elements (simple basic chemicals) are essential for plant growth. With the exception

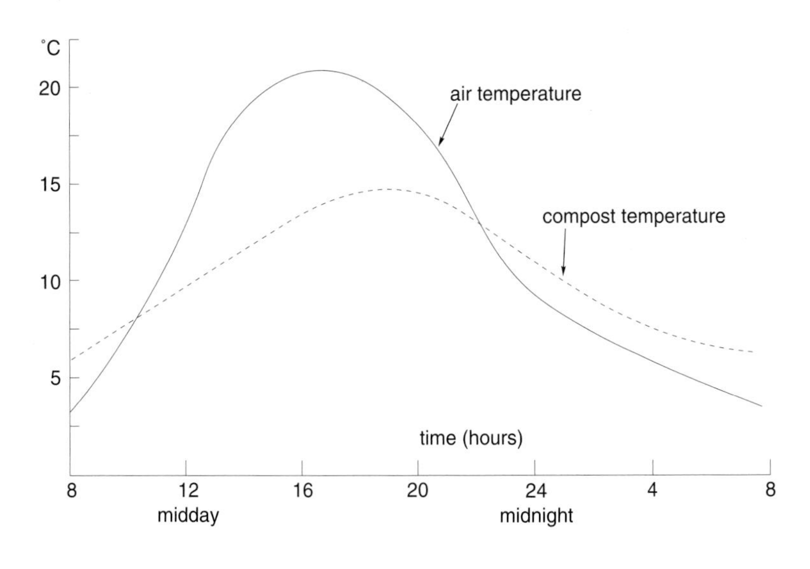

29 The air and compost temperature changes during a 24 hour period on a spring day inside a well ventilated greenhouse

of carbon all these elements enter the plant, as mineral salts, through the root. Soil water is a very weak solution of mineral salts, and as this flows to the leaves it takes the minerals with it. The plant then uses the minerals to make material for growth.

Most of the essential minerals are present in soils and composts in abundance. If any minerals are in short supply plant growth is restricted. Adding these as fertilisers restores normal growth. The three elements most likely to be in short supply are nitrogen (N), phosphorus (P) and potassium (K). Fertilisers and feeds which carry the label 'complete' contain these three chemicals.

Some elements are used in minute amounts, these are called 'trace elements' or 'micro-nutrients'. Many feeds contain these elements as they are essential for the health of the plants.

Acidity & Alkalinity

The pH scale, which measures alkalinity and acidity, is not a linear one, a movement of one on the scale represents a ten-fold change. For example a pH of 4 is ten times more acid than a pH of 5 and a hundred times more acid than a pH of 6.

A plant will not thrive if the pH of the soil is too high or too low. When added to a compost, calcium (present in lime) raises the pH and makes it less acid. It is more difficult to make a compost acidic. Plants that require a low pH (ie azeleas and some heathers) should be grown in an acid (ericaceous) compost.

The pH of a compost is measured with a kit available from garden centres. The type with a solution and a colour chart is more accurate than one with a pointer on a scale. (This does not apply to expensive scientific pH meters).

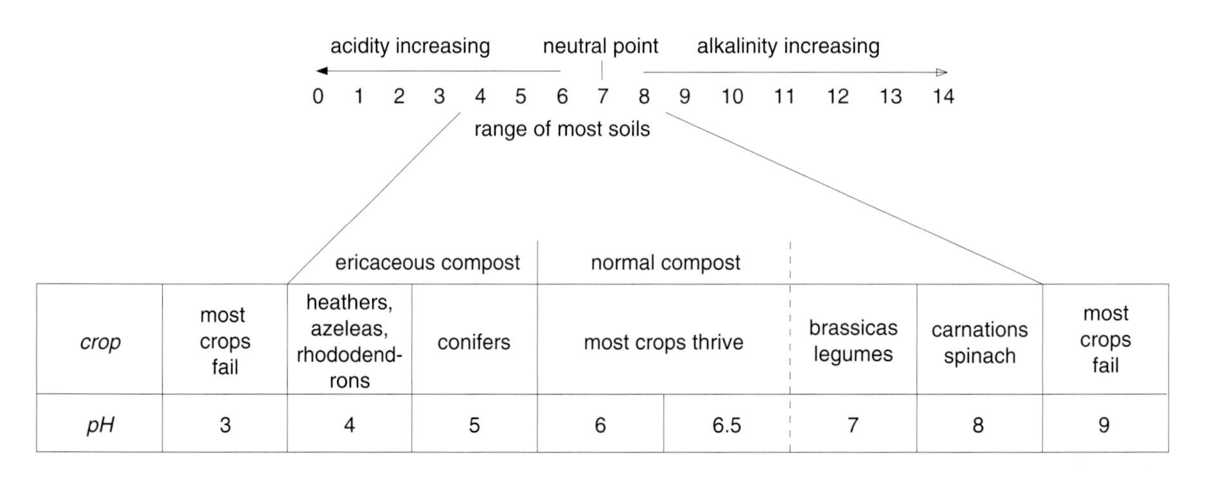

crop	most crops fail	heathers, azeleas, rhododendrons	conifers	most crops thrive		brassicas legumes	carnations spinach	most crops fail
pH	3	4	5	6	6.5	7	8	9

30 Different plants have different pH requirements

3

Raising & Caring For Plants

Composts

A soil which supports perfectly good plants in the garden is quite useless when used in a confined space such as a plant pot or plant tray. The growing medium which is used in plant pots is called 'compost' and is quite different from the compost of the compost heap. In this book the word compost always refers to the growing medium.

The compost must provide the following:

- An anchorage for plant roots.
- A good supply of water.
- Plenty of air around the root with connections through to the atmosphere.
- The correct pH level (ie the acidity of the compost).
- A good supply of major nutrients (referred to as 'plant food' elsewhere in this book).
- A full range of micro-nutrients (the chemicals which are essential to plant health but only used in tiny amounts — sometimes called trace-elements).

There are two groups of composts, those which contain soil and those which do not.

Soil Composts

These were researched many years ago by the John Innes Research Institute and are therefore called John Innes composts (JI).

John Innes composts do not store well as some chemicals in them break down to form ammonia which is harmful to plants. They can however be made at home. The ingredients are:

Loam This is produced by stacking turf upside down, covering it with black plastic to prevent weed growth and leaving it for a year. (Good

31 Mixing John Innes compost

Recipes for John Innes Composts

Seed Compost:	2 parts loam
	1 part peat
	1 part coarse sand (or substitute)
	1 gram per litre superphosphate
Potting Compost:	7 parts loam
	3 parts peat
	2 parts coarse sand (or substitute)

To this mixture add:
for *Number 1* compost 3 grams per litre of JI base. Usefor pricking out delicate seedlings
for *Number 2* compost 6 grams per litre of JI base. Use for general purpose work
for *Number 3* compost 9 grams per litre of JI base. Use for plants which make rapid growth, eg tomatoes.

All parts are by volume. A two-gallon bucket holds about 10 litres and makes a useful measure. If large quantities are to be made it may be worthwhile making a measuring box with the internal dimensions of 50cm long, 20cm wide and 10 cm deep. When level full this holds exactly 10 litres.

riddled topsoil is a viable alternative to loam). Ideally the loam should be sterilised to destroy weed seeds, soil pests and fungus diseases. See page 30.

Peat Granulated sphagnum moss peat is the most suitable. Leaf mould is a possible alternative to peat, this is made by stacking a cubic metre of autumn leaves in a surround of chicken wire. Decay to mould takes about fifteen months.

Sand The sand must be coarse with no fine material. On no account should builders' sand be used, it is too fine; nor sand from the beach, it is too salty.

Sand can be replaced with Perlite* or *Vermiculite which are easily obtainable and are very much lighter.

Chalk or Slaked Lime A small quantity may be needed to reduce the acidity of the loam.

John Innes Base This provides the compost with the essential plant nutrients and is a mixture of:
hoof & horn two parts, superphosphate two parts, potassium sulphate one part.

John Innes base is available ready mixed, there are also alternatives like Vitax — see the

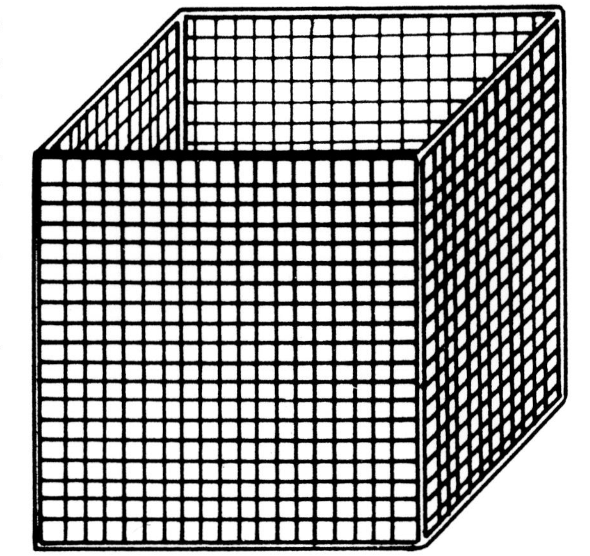

32 *A leaf mould cage*

---

* Perlite is an Italian volcanic rock which has been expanded by heating.
* Vermiculite is mined in USA and is expanded by heating. Vermiculite is less stable than Perlite and breaks down in its second year. When buying Vermiculite care should be taken to get the horticultural grade. Industrial Vermiculite is alkaline and may have been treated with a water repellant.

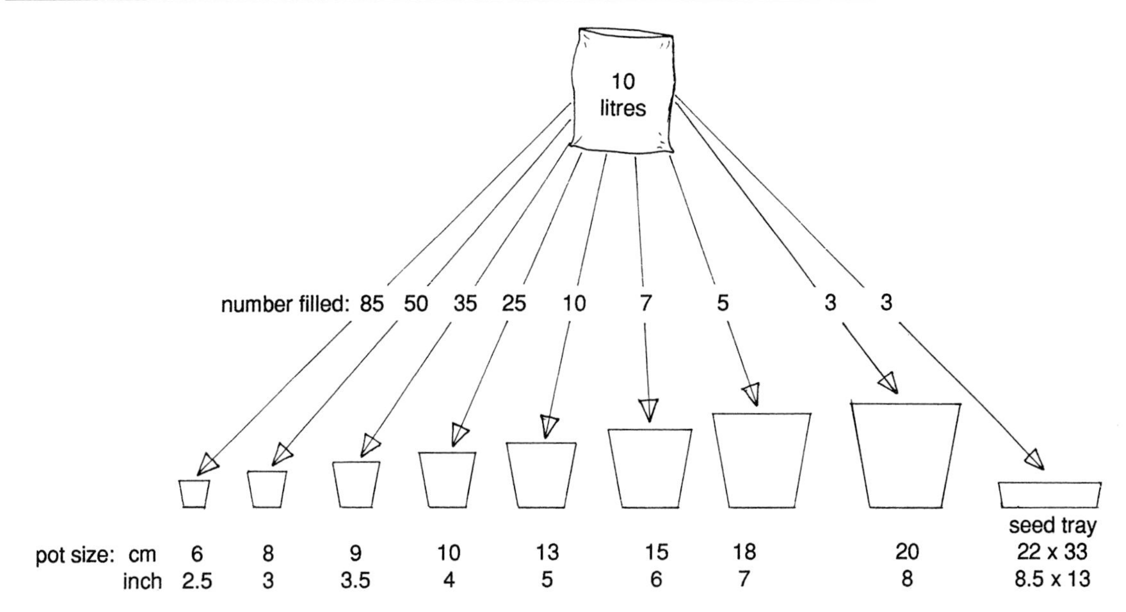

33 Diagram showing how many pots 10 litres of compost will fill — use it to calculate the quantity of compost to buy

Reference Section for suppliers.

There are two types of John Innes composts, one for sowing seeds and one for growing plants. (The plant compost is numbered 1, 2 or 3 according to the amount of nutrient it contains).

Composts should be mixed on a clean concrete floor with a clean spade or shovel.

No-Soil Composts

John Innes composts are heavy to handle and their main ingredient, good loam, is not easy to obtain. For these reasons John Innes composts have been largely replaced by no-soil composts.

Research has produced some excellent peat-only composts which, in addition to growing good plants, are light in weight, odourless and pleasant to handle. Unfortunately these composts have been so successful that peat extraction is now threatening whole ecosystems. The main alternatives to peat are bark and wastes from the coconut and chocolate industries. There is now a wide range of soilless composts both with and without peat. Virtually all soilless composts give good results, providing the grower is aware of the small differences in growing and watering techniques described elsewhere in this book.

Home-Made Soilless Compost

Soilless composts can be made at home with a certain amount of cost saving. There is no need to sterilise any of the ingredients, but mixing should be done on a clean floor. Sphagnum moss peat gives best results (Finnish peat is claimed to be forming more quickly than its rate of extraction). The peat should be slightly dampened and spread on the floor to a depth of around 15cm (6in). The fertilisers are sprinkled as evenly as possible over the surface and then the compost is thoroughly mixed with a clean spade.

A recipe for home-made soiless compost is:

sphagnum moss peat	100 litres
ammonium nitrate	40g
superphosphate	150g
potassium nitrate	70g
magnesium lime	300g
ground limestone	300g
fritted trace elements	35g

The fritted trace elements are obtainable from Garden Direct or Vitax. These companies also sell ready-mixed fertilisers for no-soil composts. A ready-mixed base is recommended as, in addition to being much easier, a single weigh-

34 A few of the commercially-available composts

ing is likely to be more accurate than six individual ones.

Note that some heathers, azeleas and some other plants thrive only in acidic soil conditions. If these are being grown the magnesium lime and ground limestone must be reduced to 50g. An acid compost, known as ericaceous, can be purchased from garden shops and centres.

Soil Sterilisation

When using soil in beds and composts, the greenhouse gardener meets two problems:

- After two or three years the soil in a greenhouse bed may become 'sick' and fail to produce a satisfactory crop. There are several causes for this including the build-up of pests and diseases.
- Soil (or loam) may contain weed seeds, pests and diseases. This can cause problems or even complete failure when used in compost.

Both these problems can be overcome by sterilising the soil. Sterilised soil is not sterile, it has been treated with either heat or chemicals to remove some bacteria, weed seeds, viruses and fungii.

There are several methods of soil sterilisation available to the commercial grower, including steam ploughs, which inject steam into the soil and propane heaters, in which soil falls down a drum which rotates around a propane flame.

There is no satisfactory method for sterilising soil beds available to the amateur grower. The best thing to do is to remove the soil and substitute fresh, although with deep-rooted plants like tomatoes, disease viruses could be present in the subsoil. An alternative is to use growbags or other methods described on page 80. Soil beds are easier to water than growbags and usually produce a better crop.

Providing that there are no weed seeds present, unsterilised loam may make good compost. There are risks that it may contain harmful organisms and diseases — but it may not!

Methods for sterilising small quantities of soil or loam:

- ***A Purpose-Built Electric Steriliser*** — This is an expensive but very effective method, the soil

35 *A soil steriliser manufactured by Thermoforce Ltd*

must be moist and care must be taken to reach, but not exceed, the required temperature. Once the temperature reaches 85°C (120°F) midway between the plates, the electricity must be turned off.

• ***Low Pressure Steam*** — On a very small scale, a thin layer of loam is spread on a clean surface, boiling water is poured over and then covered with a plastic sheet to retain the heat.

• ***Oven Method*** — Three-quarters fill a roasting bag with soil. Place it in an oven at the lowest setting and leave for one hour.
or
Microwave on high for three minutes. (Make sure that the roasting bag is not made of aluminium foil.)

• ***Chemical sterilisation***
To chemically sterilise 500 litres of soil:

1 Pour half a litre (one pint) of 40% formaldehyde into a drum which contains 20 litres (4.5 gal) of clean water.

2 Spread a layer of soil over approximately a square metre (square yard) of clean concrete to a depth of 15 cm (6 inches).

3 Apply the solution from the drum with a watering can until the soil is soaked.

4 Put a second layer on top and treat in the same way.

5 Continue with a third and fourth layer.

6 Cover the heap with a plastic sheet and leave it for forty-eight hours.

7 Remove the sheet to allow the formaldehyde to escape.

8 Five weeks later the compost is ready to use.

36 *These two plants have been treated in exactly the same way except that one has been regularly fed and the other has not (see overleaf)*

Feeding Plants

Plants use about sixteen different elements to build their tissues. Some are used in large amounts — macro-nutrients and some are used in extremely minute amounts — micro-nutrients or 'trace elements'. If any of these is in short supply the growth and development of the plant will suffer. Shortages of nutrients are corrected by adding chemical fertilisers. Gardeners call this 'feeding'.

The three elements which are most often in short supply are nitrogen, phosphorous (phosphate) and potassium (potash). These elements affect the plant in different ways.

A complete fertiliser will state the proportions of nitrogen, phosphate and potash it contains.

These proportions are given as single numbers like this: 10:5:8 which means 10 per cent nitrogen, 5 per cent phosphate and 8 per cent potash. A good fertiliser will contain other nutrients and trace elements as well. Badly fed plants are more likely to suffer from pests and diseases than well fed ones.

37 Fertilisers are available for all types of plants

The Effects Of Nitrogen, Phosporous & Potassium on Plants

Element	*Part most affected*	*Signs of shortage*	*Effect of adding too much*
Nitrogen	leaves	yellow colour leaves	Rank, spindly growth, delayed maturity
Phosphate	roots	poor growth blue colour on leaves	effects not easily seen
Potash	flowers and fruit	leaf margins die	new growth small and tinted with blue

Feeding Greenhouse Plants

1. Select two complete fertilisers from the large number that is available in garden shops. One which is high in nitrogen (eg 20:10:10) and one which is high in potash (eg 15:15:30)
2. Check feeding instructions on compost bags and growbags as different types of composts have different feeding requirements.
3. Begin feeding in early spring as growth commences and feed as a routine on a certain day each week. Use the high nitrogen feed..
4. Add the feed to the normal watering strictly in accordance with the manufacturer's instructions. **Do not overfeed** and do not feed very dry plants — water them first.
5. When fruit and flowers begin to appear, change over to the high potash feed (a good time to do this is when the first truss of tomatoes is fully set)

Watering Plants in Pots & Trays

The success of the greenhouse gardener depends largely on his or her skill at watering. The amounts of water needed vary according to the weather, the time of year and the plant type and stage of growth. Most greenhouse plants should not be watered until there are signs of dryness, the skill is to recognising a plant's need for water before it wilts, as wilting reduces growth.

Signs that the compost in a plant pot or tray may be dry are:

- The surface of the compost looks dry. (This does not apply to some coir composts — a very dry surface may cover a very wet compost).
- The compost is shrinking from the edge of the pot.
- The pot, or tray feels lighter than an obviously wet one.
- The compost is dry to the touch.
- The plant is wilting.
- If the pot is clay a tap with the knuckles produces a high ring.

A greenhouse plant may also be too wet and this may cause the death of a plant.

Signs that the compost in a plant pot or tray may be too wet are:

- The surface of the compost looks wet.
- The surface of the compost appears sealed with no apparent air passages.
- The pot, or tray feels heavy compared with a normal one.
- The compost is wet to the touch.
- The plant is wilting.
- Patches of seedlings are collapsing and mould is present.
- If the pot is clay, tapping with the knuckles produces a dull thud.

Note that sometimes the surface of the compost around a pot plant becomes coated with algae, this can be corrected by gently stirring the surface with a pointed stick. Better still it can be prevented by a layer of chippings or similar on the surface of the compost.

Checking the Effectiveness of Watering

1. Water the plants in your normal way
2. Wait for half an hour
3. Take two pot plants from the back of the bench, two from the middle and two from the front
4. Knock the plants from their pots and examine the rootballs for moisture
5. Return the plants to their pots

Rain water or mains water can be used for greenhouse watering. Mains water can be used straight from the tap, or from a previously filled tub which is kept inside the greenhouse. The water in the tub is often a little warmer than straight from the tap, but this advantage is probably outweighed by the presence of algae and the possibility of bacterial and fungal contamination. If a tub is used it should be kept covered and cleaned regularly.

A Haws-type watering can is probably the most suitable for a greenhouse, it is well balanced and the long spout makes reaching plants at the back of the staging an easy matter.

A rose should always be used for seeds and seedlings, extra care must be taken not to over wet seedlings or they may collapse with a fungus disease — 'damping off'. Large plants in pots are watered without a rose, the water is applied directly but gently to the surface of the compost and the foliage kept dry. The final stage of watering is to thoroughly wet the greenhouse floor, this is called 'damping down'. Damping down increases the humidity of the greenhouse and reduces the amount of water the plants will lose. Damping down is also a good method of reducing the temperature of the greenhouse on very hot days. Damping down is not done in winter, nor on cold humid autumn days, as a dry atmosphere is helpful in the control of fungus diseases.

38 Rain water is better than tap water for orchids, some heathers and other plants which grow in acid soil

39 The large watering can is used in summer and the small one in winter; this helps to prevent getting compost too wet in winter

Plants in the greenhouse are entirely dependant upon the greenhouse gardener for their water supply. Too much water and the plant dies, too little and the plant also dies. It is

40 This plant has been over-watered and an attempt is being made to restore it

however easier to correct under-watering than over-watering. A plant with too little water will wilt, a *recently* wilted plant will soon recover with a good watering. A pot plant that has been over-watered is difficult to dry out, specially if it is growing in a plastic pot and peat compost. One method that sometimes works, is to tap the plant out of its pot and stand it on several sheets of dry newspaper. Return the plant to its pot a few days later.

Drying out may also be assisted by gently stirring the surface of the compost with a small stick. The roots of a waterlogged plant cannot obtain enough oxygen, this causes them to turn brown and die.

Although watering is a daily job not every plant will need watering every day. A good rule for plants growing in a soil based compost is to leave them until they are fairly dry (but not wilting) and then give them sufficient water to wet all the compost in the pot. This is done by filling the space on top of the compost with water. This treatment does not work too well with soilless composts for two reasons:

- Soilless composts hold a lot of water and soon become too wet.

- When soilless composts are very dry they may be difficult to wet.

Little and often is a better rule for plants in soilless compost. The way in which pots are filled can aid good watering; when potting with

41 The plastic bottle makes watering growbags easy, while the wooden surround keeps the compost at a better depth

a soilless compost fill the pot almost to the top. This prevents a large volume of water from lying on the surface and soaking down into an already wet root ball. When potting with a soil based compost leave a centimetre (half an inch) or so unfilled, this space is then available to fill with water.

During winter plants use much less water than they do in summer but most need a little. Over-watering is very likely to occur in winter, a small can should be used and the compost kept only slightly moist.

Watering growbags can be difficult especially in high summer when they are supporting lots of foliage. A plastic lemonade bottle, with the bottom cut off, makes watering easier and allows a larger volume to be applied at each watering.

The compost in a very dry growbag can be difficult to wet, a little washing-up liquid added to the water may help.

Capillary Matting.

Capillary matting is a felt-like material that soaks up and holds water. A good matting will hold three litres of water per square metre (almost five pints per square yard). If a waterproof *level* bench is covered with capillary matting and one end is immersed in a tank of water, just below bench level, the matting will remain wet. Any water lost from the matting will be replaced by soaking up free water from the

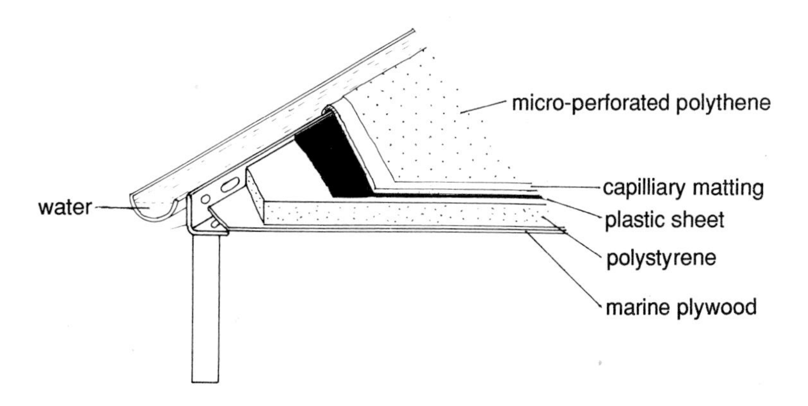

42 A home-made capilliary bench. Some gardeners use a split water pipe instead of a gutter in order to control algae

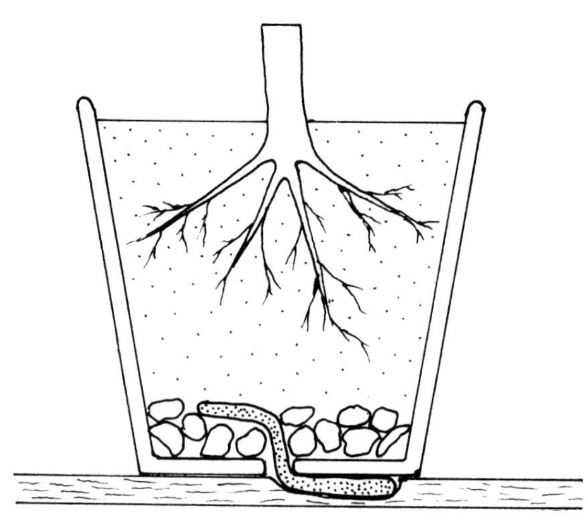

43 A wick connection between the compost and the capillary matting is necessary for clay pots

tank. If the tank is kept filled with a ball valve or a 'glug' bottle, the matting on the bench will be permanently wet.

Standing plant pots and trays on permanently wet capillary matting removes the need for watering. This method has been tried and tested in commercial nurseries and satisfactory small scale models can be made by a handy person.

When pots or trays are first placed on the matting, they may need a little water applied to the top of the compost for a day or two. Once water is being taken up from the matting there is no need to water with a can.

Hosepipes

During the summer months, high temperatures, long days and lots of foliage all increase the plants' water requirement. Under these conditions it is possible to make use of a hosepipe for some of the watering in a greenhouse. Extreme care must be taken not to wash compost from the pots or to splash soil on the foliage and fruit. A jet of water from an open ended hose can damage the structure of the soil in greenhouse beds. Ideally the hosepipe should be fitted with a rose and the water pressure kept fairly low.

Trouble Shooting Problems with Capillary Matting:

Problem	*Solution*
Some plants need to dry out between waterings eg pelargoniums & succulents	Do not use a capillary bench for these plants
As there is no drainage fertilisers may build up to harmful levels in the compost	Water from the top every two weeks or so to correct this
Algae grows on the surface of the matting	Cover with plastic and cut holes for pots and trays. *or* Cover with micro-perforated polythene *or* Water on a chemical algae killer (algicide)
Roots grow from the bottom of pots into the matting. When moved the roots are broken and the plant checked.	Cover the matting with micro-perforated polythene, this material does not impare capillary action and it reduces evaporation.
Clay pots have a single hole and do not take water from the bed.	Make a wick from a strip of capillary matting and thread it through the hole. See diagram above.
A capillary bed makes plants too wet in winter.	Do not use in winter.

Trickle Irrigation

Trickle systems supply water from a reservoir directly to soil beds, containers or growbags, through a series of small bore tubes. The nozzles on the ends of the tubes may, or may not, be adjustable. A trickle system can also be used to keep a capillary bed supplied with water.

Several systems are available, each with different detail but a similar principle. A typical system is shown in the diagram.

Before setting up a system it is very useful to know how much water is being given to each plant daily. A container is placed under each nozzle to measure how much water is being delivered, each nozzle can then be adjusted to give the correct flow rate. Water requirements of plants differ with the weather, so set the nozzles to deliver dull day requirements and top up with a watering can on hot days. This will prevent over-watering.

Seep Hoses

A seep hose is a hosepipe with very small perforations along its length. It is laid flat on a soil bed or threaded through a growbag and connected to a water supply. Water gradually seeps from the hose to maintain water levels. A seep hose can cause waterlogging and it should be adjusted to deliver dull day requirements; extra should be given from a watering can on bright days.

A seep hose can be fitted with a valve which opens when the soil is dry and closes when it is wet. A sensor is placed in the soil to operate the valve, and if this is in the correct position the system becomes automatic.

Overhead Spraylines

A plastic waterpipe is suspended along the length of the greenhouse about 30cm (1ft) below the roof. Spray heads are fitted into this pipe at regular intervals. Mains water is connected, this breaks into a fine spray and falls to the floor.

The system is often used in large greenhouses where tomatoes are grown in soil beds. Once the first truss of tomatoes has set the sprayline is lowered to 0.5 metres (1ft 6in) from the soil. A sprayline is unsuitable for plant pots and growbags. Another problem is that tender plants will collapse under the weight of water being delivered.

Although commercial growers use spraylines for lettuce and other crops, the amateur greenhouse gardener is advised to use other watering methods.

44 A trickle system in use

Mist (see page 51)

Trays of small seeds can be difficult to water, especially if the gardener is in a hurry.

If placed under a mist propagator they will remain constantly moist and unlikely to damp off (see page 102).

It is important to remove the trays of seeds as soon as they have germinated.

45 One of the heads on a spray line

Propagation from Seeds

A seed consists of a protective coat, covering a tiny plant and a food store. When given water, air and warmth the tiny plant is nourished by the food store and begins to grow. This process is called 'germination'. Most seeds will germinate in darkness but a few require light.

Seeds are sown in either a seed compost or a multi-purpose compost; if a potting compost is used there is a danger that the fertilisers present will damage the seeds during their first stages of germination. **It is important that containers are correctly filled, as it is false economy to save compost by only half filling them.** This is probably the commonest mistake made by amateur gardeners.

Primed Seed

Some seed suppliers offer 'primed seed'. These seeds have been brought to the point of germination and held in that state. Primed seeds germinate more quickly and more evenly than unprimed seeds, especially at temperatures which are lower than ideal. Seedlings from unprimed seeds soon catch up and after a few weeks there is no obvious difference. Growers who have difficulty in germinating some types of seeds may find the extra cost of primed seeds worthwhile.

46 Filling a seed tray with compost

47 Ensure that the corners are properly filled

48 Level the compost using a board

49 Gently firm the compost

50 Always use a correctly written label

TAGETES orange gem March 19

51 Water the compost with a fine rose

52 Sow the seeds evenly over the compost

53 Cover the seeds with an even layer of compost with a sieve

Sowing Small Seeds

1 Select a tray or shallow pot according to the amount of seed you wish to sow. (These instructions now refer to a tray, the process with a pot is the same.)

2 Pile compost over the tray.

3 Press compost into the corners to make sure that these are properly filled.

4 Remove the surplus compost by pushing a board across the tray. This leaves the tray level full.

5 Gently firm the compost with a board (or the bottom of a second tray). This leaves the surface about 5mm (a quarter inch) below the top of the tray.

6 Water the compost with a fine rose and allow it to drain. (This can be speeded up by covering the tray with a board and holding sidewards for a few minutes).

7 Write a label with the type of seed and the date. Use a pen which is both waterproof and *lightproof*. Start writing from the blunt end of the label.

8 If the seeds are large enough to handle, place them evenly over the compost in five rows of eight, this will save the need to prick out later. If the seeds are small, tip them on to a piece of strong white paper. Hold the paper above the compost and dislodge the seeds by gently tapping the edge of the paper. Distribute the seeds evenly over the compost. Do not sow too thickly or the seedlings will become tall and spindly and are much more likely to damp off.

9 Use a sieve (not too fine) to cover the seeds with an even layer of compost. Small seeds need only a light cover, just enough so they cannot be seen. Very small seeds like begonia or lobelia should not be covered, a smart tap on the side of the tray will shake them into the compost. Large seeds should be covered with a layer of compost which is twice the width of the seed. Some seeds require light, these should not be covered but pressed into the surface with a board or a second tray.

10 Stick the label upright in the centre of the tray. Slide the tray into a large polythene bag and leave the end open. The label keeps the plastic above the compost. Shade from direct sunlight with a sheet of newspaper or coloured plastic.

11 Follow either a, or b, or c.

a Leave the tray of seeds in the greenhouse to germinate.

b Put the tray inside a propagator and set the temperature (for most seeds 18-25°C/65-75°F). Nearly all seeds will germinate at lower temperatures but they will take longer and the risk of failure will increase. Some seeds (eg hardy primulas) will not germinate at these high temperatures and should be placed in a cool part of the greenhouse or left outside with some protection.

c Germinate the seeds inside the house. As soon as the seedlings appear transfer them to the greenhouse.

12 Inspect the tray at least once a day and as soon as the seedlings can be seen remove the tray from the bag.

13 Prick out the seedlings as soon as possible and certainly before the first true leaf appears.

Pricking out Seedlings

Seedlings, produced by the method just described, do not have enough space to develop. They soon become tall, spindly and quite useless as plants.

Each seedling must be given space to grow, this is done by digging them up and replanting them individually in pots or spaced out in seed trays. Transplanting seedlings is known as pricking out.

Seedlings should be pricked out as soon as they are large enough to handle.

54 Seedlings in between these two stages of development are ideal for pricking out

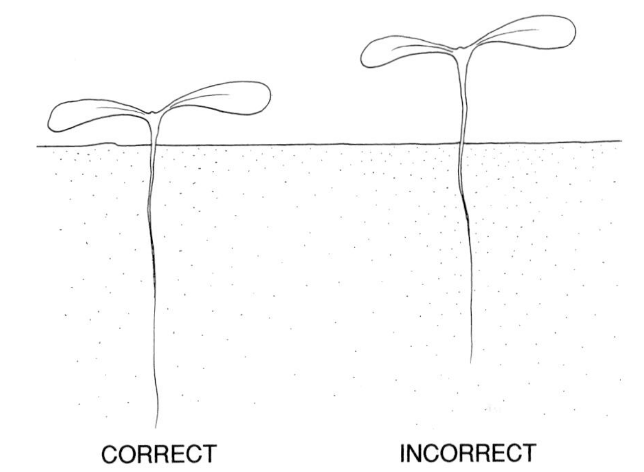

55 Correctly and incorrectly placed seedlings

Pricking out Seedlings

1 Fill a plant tray with **potting** compost in exactly the same way as shown for sowing seeds.
2 Gently firm the compost and water with a rose can. The compost should be damp but not waterlogged.
3 Write a label. (Include the date the seeds were sown.)
4 On the compost mark the position of the plants in the top row and the left-hand side row. Eight rows of four plants and ten rows of five plants are common populations for a standard seed tray.
5 Take a small dibber (no larger than a pencil) and gently dig up a clump of seedlings.
6 From this clump tease out a single seedling, holding it carefully by a leaf. A seedling should never be held by the stem — it can grow a new leaf but not a new stem!
7 Using the dibber make a hole in the compost at the top left corner of the tray. Insert the seedling and gently firm the compost around it.
8 Complete the top row, follow on with the left hand row then complete each row in turn. Care must be taken to put only one seedling at each station — although lobelia is pricked out as small bunches of seedlings.
9 Place the tray of seedlings on the staging in good light, but avoid direct sunlight for a few days.

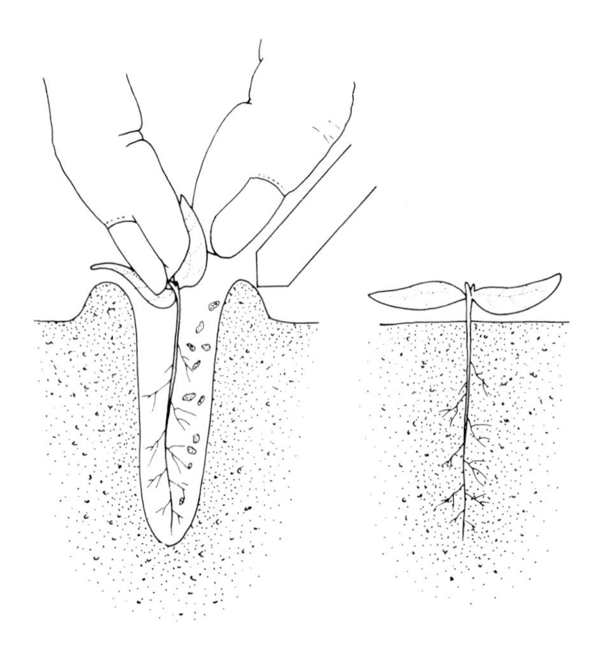

56 The correct method of inserting a seedling into the compost

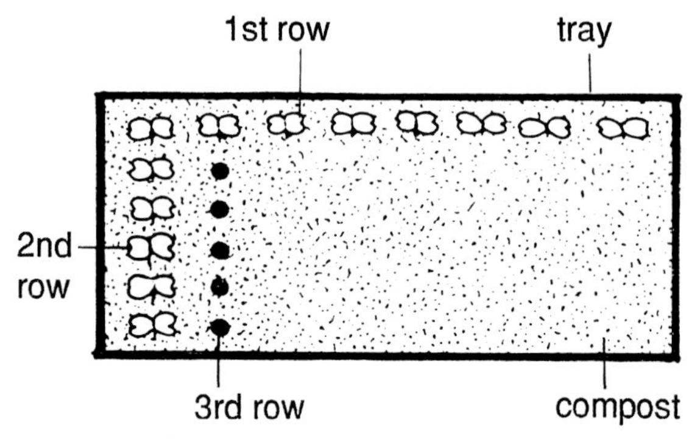

57 A tray of seedlings showing the position of the rows and the sequence of work

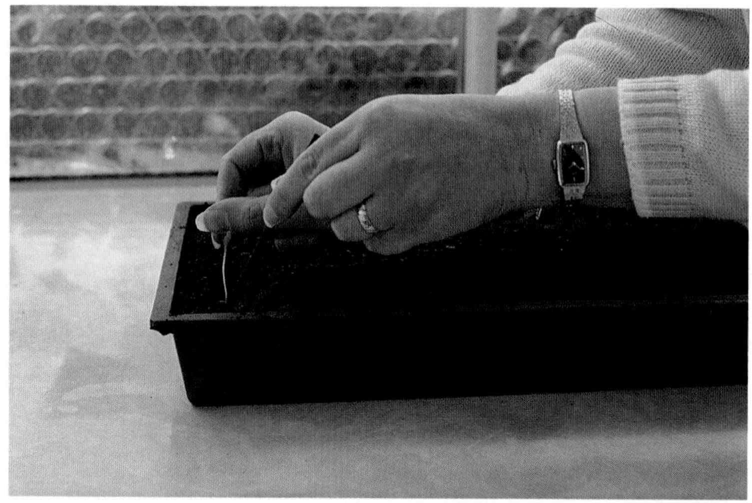

58 Pricking out seedlings

59 Seedlings pricked out into root trainers (left) and a plant tray (right)

Potting Up

Seedlings of tomatoes, peppers and many house plants are pricked out directly into pots, this process is referred to as 'potting up'. Seedlings are not potted up into their final pots straight away, they are moved from small pots into larger pots as they develop.

There are two reasons for this:

- Small pots take less space making better use of the greenhouse.
- A plant grown in.this way has a better root system than one which started life in its final pot.

Note: when potting up seedlings with a soil based compost fill the pot 5mm (¼in) below the rim of the pot. When using a soilless compost fill the pot almost to the brim — this will aid watering.

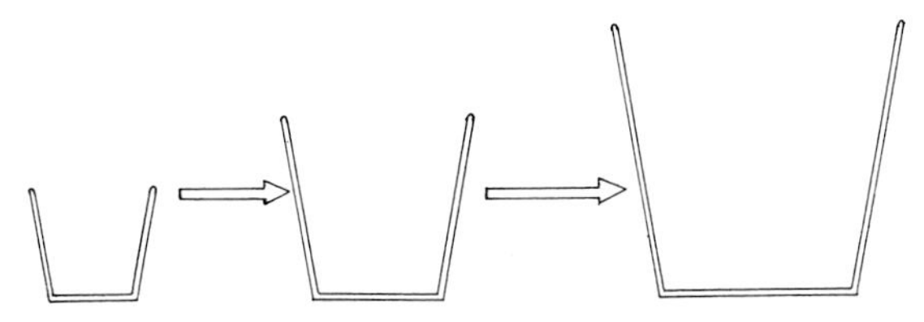

60 During its development a plant is grown in a number of different pots, each larger than its predecessor

Potting On

Transferring a potplant into a larger pot is known as 'potting on'.

61 (right) Removing a plant from its pot

Potting On

1. Water the plants which are to be potted on and leave to stand for half an hour.
2. Put a layer of compost into the bottom of the larger pot and place the plant, pot and all, onto it. Add or remove compost until the brims of the two pots are level.
3. Knock out the plant from its pot as shown. If the roots are coiling around the bottom, gently tease them out.
4. Place the plant centrally in the new pot.
5. Fill the space around the sides with new compost and gently firm the new compost. Do not apply any pressure to the old root ball, or the roots may be damaged.

   Note: Some soilless composts require very light compaction.
6. Water with care and place on the staging to grow.

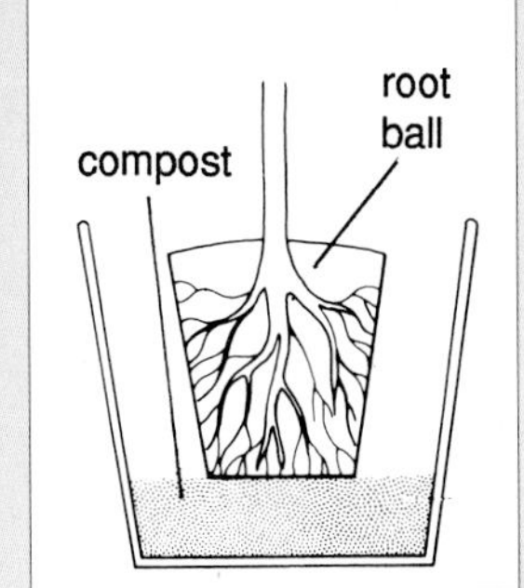

62 The plant in position

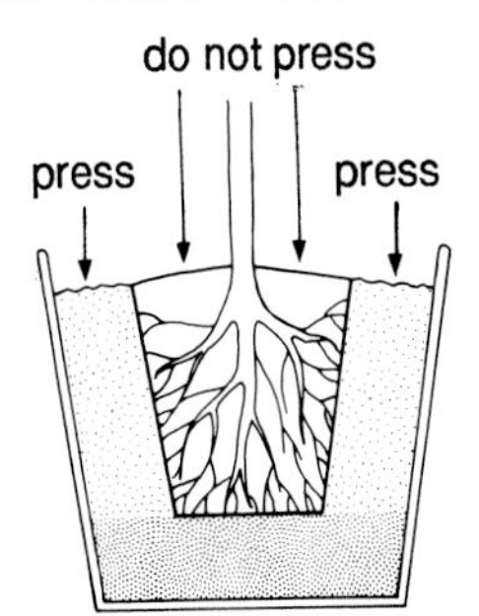

63 Firming the compost

Cuttings

If part of a plant is removed and kept in certain conditions it may grow and develop into a new plant. In this way several plants can be propagated from one parent plant. Plants raised by this method will have exactly the same characteristics as the parent plant. The part which is taken from the parent plant is called a cutting.

There are several different types of cutting, some plants propagate easily from a stem cutting, whilst others are best propagated from a leaf or bud. To find out which type to use for a particular plant refer to later sections of this chapter and to Chapter 4.

Conditions which aid the development are:

- A temperature suitable for plant growth.
- A good supply of oxygen to the part where the roots will grow from.
- A good supply of water.
- A humid atmosphere which keeps water stress to a minimum.
- The absence of bacteria and fungus which cause disease.
- A supply of auxins (hormones) to the cut part.
- Good light — *but not direct sunlight.*

The Rooting Medium

The compost in which a cutting is placed is called a 'rooting medium'. This medium must have lots of air spaces, hold water and have no disease organisms. It must have only a very small amount of nitrogen fertiliser present — or none at all. Once cuttings have formed roots they will require a supply of nitrogen. This can be given as a light feed or by using a container with rooting medium at the top and potting compost at the bottom.

There are many different kinds of rooting mediums, one of the most successful which can be made at home is: equal parts of fine grade Cambark and medium grade sphagnum moss peat, mixed together.

Another one is: equal parts of a multi-purpose compost and Perlite mixed together.

Either of these rooting mediums can be used for the cuttings which are described on the next few pages.

Rooting Powder & Rooting Gel

Rooting powder or rooting gel (obtainable from all garden shops and centres) contain a plant hormone which aids success as it speeds up rooting.

The cut end is coated in powder by dipping in and shaking off the surplus. The cutting should not be dipped into the container as the powder may become wet and spoil. A very small quantity tipped into the lid is ideal for dipping and any surplus can be discarded.

Parent Plants

Cutings from young vigorously growing plants root much better than those from older plants.

Older shrubs will produce good material for cuttings if one or two branches on the south side are pruned hard.

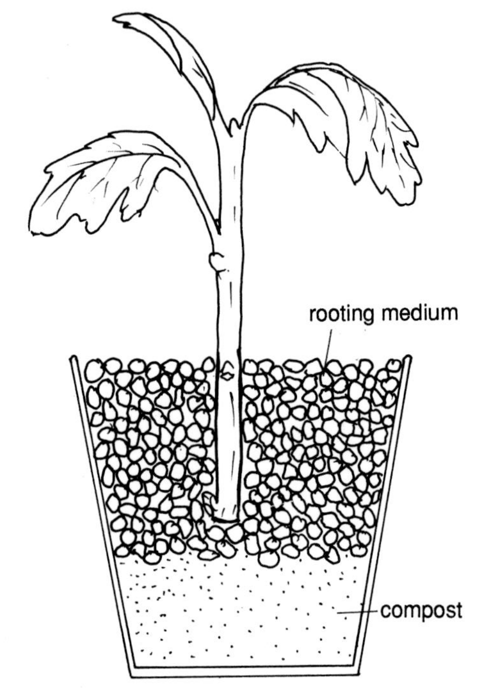

64 This cutting will be 'fed' as its roots reach the compost

Propagating by Softwood Cuttings:

1 Select a container which is well drained and at least 10cm (4 inches) deep. A 12 cm (5 inch) pot will take five cuttings, root trainers will take up to fifty.

2 Fill the container with rooting medium and firm this by lifting the container a couple of centimetres (an inch) or so and dropping it onto the bench. Do not press the medium down as this reduces the amount of air.

3 Water with a rose can and leave to drain.

4 Select young vigorous shoots near to the base of the plant rejecting any with flower buds. Cut off around 10cm (4in) of each shoot and place them in a polythene bag.

5 Prepare each cutting by removing the bottom of the stem with a clean square cut just below a node (leaf joint). Remove any leaves and buds from the bottom half of the cutting, leaving two or three (but no more) at the top. If the lowest leaf is rather large, remove half of it.

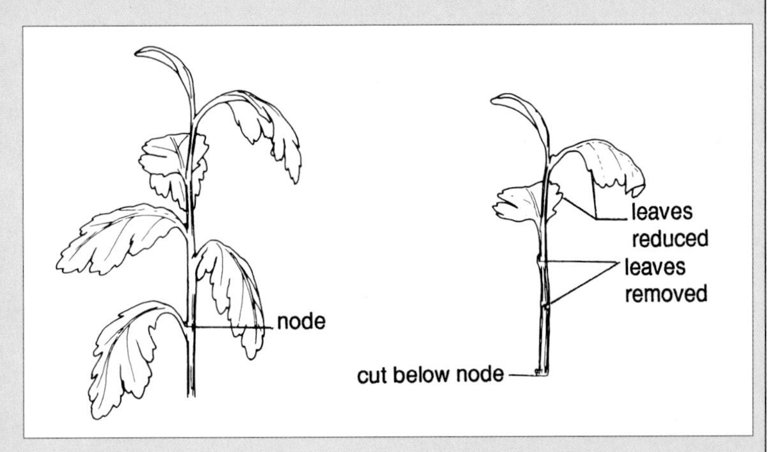

65 An unprepared (left) and a prepared cutting (right)

6 Make a hole in the medium with a small dibber, dip the lower end of the cutting into rooting powder and insert it leaving 1cm (½in) of clear stem above the medium. Fill the hole with medium and firm very gently.

7 Insert the other cuttings and push four split canes around the edge of the pot to prevent the leaves from touching plastic. Invert a plastic bag over the pot and fix with adhesive tape or a rubber band.

8 Put the pot into a warm light place, but not in direct sunlight. A propagator with bottom heat is ideal.

9 After a couple of weeks test for signs of rooting, this is done by *gently* pulling a cutting, if you feel a little resistance it means that roots are growing.

10 As soon as the cuttings have rooted open the polythene bag by slitting it across the top, do not remove it as sudden removal may cause the cuttings to collapse. Three or four days later remove the bag.

11 Pot up the cuttings in small pots and a potting compost. Grow on in the greenhouse and treat according to type.

66 Cutting in a pot, sealed with a plastic bag

Trouble Shooter — Cuttings

Problem	*Cause*	*Solution*
Cuttings turn black at the base and die.	Shortage of air in the medium.	Use a more open medium — add more grit or Perlite. Take care not to get the medium too wet.
The leaves become mouldy.	Fungus disease (botrytis).	Use sterilised medium (see pages 30-1). Make sure that the container is clean.
Cuttings appear healthy, but fail to root.	Low temperature or slow rooting species.	21°C (70°F) is best for most cuttings. Some species take longer than others.

Ten Points for Success with Softwood Cuttings

1. Take cuttings from strong vigorous growth — either from a young plant or from the new growth of an old plant which has been recently cut hard back.
2. Use a very sharp knife — and keep it sharp.
3. Use material which is completely free from pests and diseases.
4. Use vegetative shoots, ie no flower buds.
5. Insert the cutting as soon as it has been prepared. (Except for pelargoniums.)
6. Collect cutting material in a polythene bag as this reduces water loss.
7. Remove soft tips which wilt.
8. Use a hormone rooting powder to speed up rooting.
9. Do not push the cutting directly into the medium — make a hole with a dibber.
10. Make sure that the leaves are not resting directly on the surface.

67 Rooting powder being used from the lid of the container

Types of Cuttings

- ***Stem Cuttings*** — There are three types of stem cuttings, young stems (softwood), middle-aged stems (semi-hardwood) and old stems (hardwood). In practice most softwood stems are taken in spring, semi-hardwood in summer and hardwood in autumn.
- ***Semi-Hardwood Cuttings*** — Many trees and shrubs can be propagated from semi-hardwood. This type of cutting is taken from July to September when new shoots on garden shrubs are beginning to go 'woody' and harden. Cuttings of semi-hardwood are treated in the same way as those of softwood, only the method of collection and preparation is different.
- ***Hardwood Cuttings*** — Fruit trees, roses and many garden shrubs (both evergreen and deciduous) are easily propagated from hardwood cuttings. A cold greenhouse is ideal for hardwood cuttings.
- ***Conifer Cuttings*** — Most conifers are easily propagated from cuttings. A cold or a frost-free greenhouse is ideal for this purpose as the cuttings are taken in October when the summer crops have finished.
- ***Climbing Plants*** — Climbing plants (eg Clematis) have long lengths of stem in between the leaf joints, this makes 'normal' cuttings virtually impossible.
- ***Leaf Cuttings*** — A number of house plants do not have stems and these are propagated from their leaves. Although leaf cuttings can be taken at any time of the year, they are best taken in summer when the light levels are good.

The Propagation of Conifers

1. One-third fill small pots (yoghurt pots with large drainage holes cut in are ideal) with potting or multi-purpose compost. Fill to the top with Perlite, Vermiculite or very coarse sand.
2. Water well and cover the top with cling film, secure this with adhesive tape or a rubber band.
3. Use secateurs to cut off lengths of new growth including about 3cm (1in) of *brown* wood.
4. Clear the bottom 5cm (2 in) of stem by snatching off the side growths. This wounds the brown part of the stem and aids root formation.
5. Moisten the wounded end and dip it into rooting powder.
6. Make a small hole in the centre of the cling film and insert the cutting so that the end is in the centre of the pot, ie 1cm (½in) or so above the potting compost.
7. Place on the greenhouse staging and shade from direct sunlight. Some frost will not harm the cuttings but do not allow the pots to freeze solid. (see page 13 on how to avoid this)
8. The cuttings will have rooted by spring, pot them up into 8cm (3in) pots. Grow on in the greenhouse for a few weeks before hardening off for use outside.

68 An unprepared (left) and an prepared conifer cutting (right)

Propagation from Semi-Hardwood Cuttings

1 Select short lateral (side) growths that are soft at the top and hard at the bottom. Pull them away from the stem taking a small piece of old stem with them. The attached piece of old stem is called a 'heel'.

2 Remove the bottom leaves and trim the heel by removing any attached old wood and leaving the bark; trim off any straggly 'tails' of bark.

3 Imerse cuttings in a weak fungicide solution for a few seconds.

4 Proceed as for soft-wood cuttings — this type of cutting takes two or three weeks longer than soft-wood cuttings.

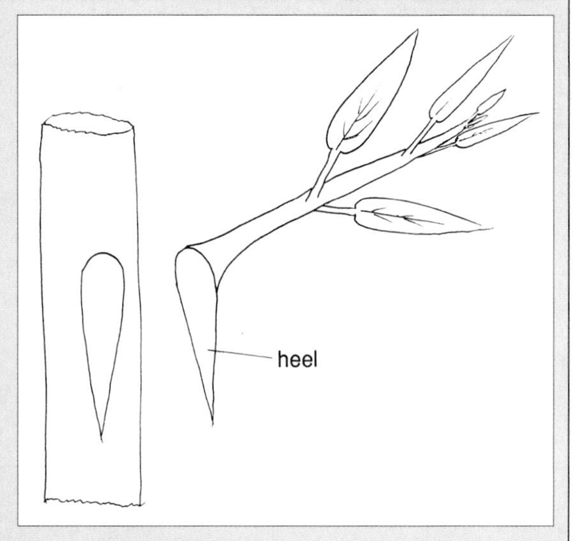

69 Cutting with a heel

Propagation From Hardwood Cuttings

1 During November collect 20-25 cm (8-10in) lengths of the current year's growth.

2 Cut off the top immature part, just *above* a bud, making a sloping cut which leaves the bud near to the top.

3 Make a square cut at the lower end, just *below* a bud.

4 Remove all the buds except for the top three. (With blackcurrants and other plants which are grown as a stool, leave all the buds on).

5 Fill 12cm (5in) full pots (Continental pots are not deep enough) with rooting medium level with the top. Make five holes in the medium with a dibber and dip the lower end of each cutting into rooting powder.

7 Imerse the cuttings in a weak fungicide for a few seconds.

8 Insert the cuttings to a depth which leaves the lowest bud 2cm (1in) above the top of the medium. The base of the cuttings must be well clear of the bottom of the pot — if this is not so, shorten them.

9 Keep in a cold greenhouse throughout the winter with the compost slightly moist but not wet.

10 If you live in a very cold district and there is a danger of the pots freezing solid, plunge them into a soil bed to prevent this.

11 Successful cuttings will begin to grow in spring, pot these up and grow-on in the usual way.

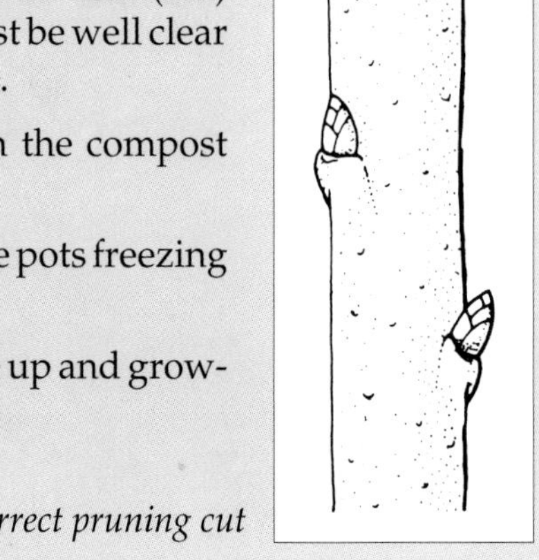

70 The correct pruning cut

The Propagation of Clematis

1 During June or July cut 5cm (2in) lengths of stem with a leaf joint in the centre of each one.

2 Cut off one of the leaves.

3 Treat in exactly the same way as softwood cuttings but insert with the buds just above the surface of the rooting medium.

Taking Leaf Cuttings

a ***Whole leaf complete with stalk,*** eg Saintpaulia (African violet), Gloxinia, small leaved Begonias and small-leaved Peperomias.

1 Take a whole leaf, complete with *all* its stalk from the plant. (If part of the stalk is left on the parent plant it becomes a site for disease to enter.)

2 Dip the end of the stalk in rooting powder and root in the way described for softwood cuttings.

b ***Whole leaf only,*** eg succulents such as Crassula, Echeveria and Sedum.

1 Remove a mature fleshy leaf and leave it to dry for three days.

2 Cover the surface of the rooting medium with 5mm (quarter inch) of sharp sand.

3 Insert 1cm (½in) of the cut end of the leaf into the medium.

4 Place in a propagator, do not cover with a plastic bag and water very sparingly.

c ***Parts of leaves,*** egBegonia Rex, Sansevieria (Mother-in-law's tongue) and Streptocarpus (Cape primrose)

1 Remove a whole leaf.

2 For Begonis rex: cut into triangles with 5cm (2 inch) sides. For the others: cut into 6cm (2½in) sections.

3 For Begonia rex: dip the tip which is furthest from the leaf edge into rooting powder.
For the others: dip the end which was nearest the plant into rooting powder.

4 Insert the cuttings vertically into the medium with half of them buried.

5 Treat in the same way as described for softwood cuttings.

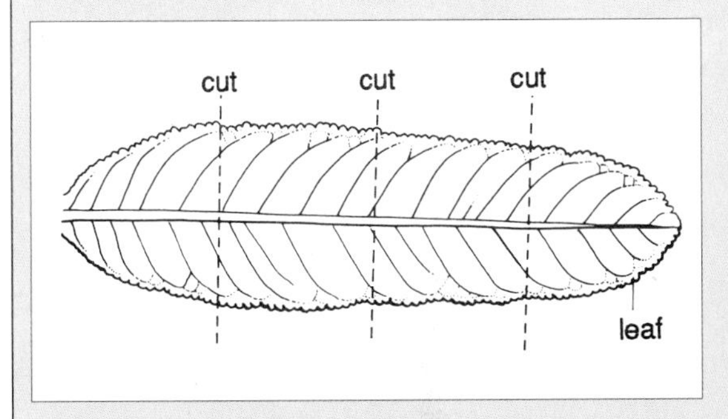

71 (left) Leaf cuttings with just part of a leaf

72 (right) Half bury the cut leaves

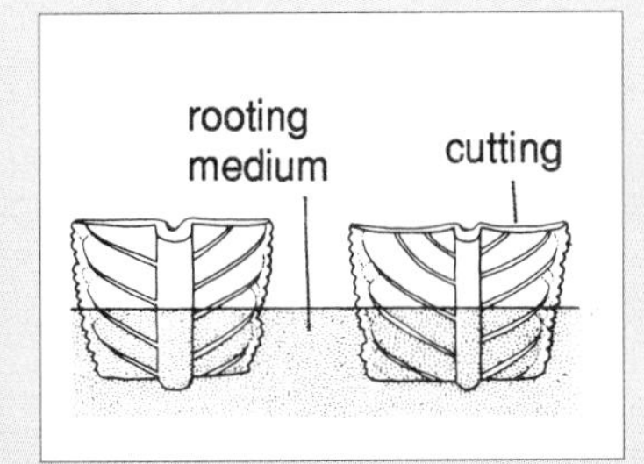

Note: Variegated Sansevieria will produce all green leaves when propagated by this method. The only way to produce daughter plants with the variegation is to remove the plant from its pot and divide it vertically through the roots. Pot up the individual parts into separate pots.

73 (above) A prepared Clematis cutting

74 (top right) Clematis cutting with the buds just above the rooting medium. It is important that the buds are in contact with the compost as this is where the roots grow from

75 Leaf cuttings of Saintpaulia (African violet) and Begonia Rex

Mist Progagation

Cuttings root more quickly and reliably when their leaves are kept permanently moist. This can be achieved in the greenhouse by spraying a very fine mist over them whenever they begin to dry out.

Water is forced through the very small hole, marked 'A', and strikes the metal plate, marked 'B', with considerable force. The impact shatters the water into tiny drops, which fall slowly as a mist. The size of the droplets is adjusted by turning the knob marked 'C'. Some mist heads are not adjustable but are pre-set to produce a very fine mist

The mist continues until there is enough water on the bare electrodes of the electronic leaf to complete a circuit; when this circuit is complete a solenoid valve turns the mist off. When the electrodes dry out, the current stops and the mist is automatically turned on again. The amount of wetting that the cuttings receive depends upon the position of the electronic leaf, this position being determined by the gardener. The more expensive misting kits have electronic devices which give considerably more control than can be achieved just by the positioning of the electronic leaf.

Mist propagation is extremely successful because:

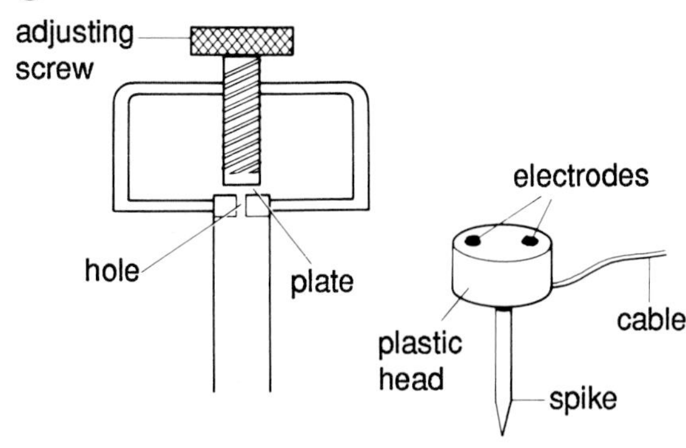

76 A mist propagator and an electronic leaf

77 (above right) A mist propagator and its controls

78 Plants hardening off in the shelter of a Robinsons greenhouse (see page 53)

• The humid atmosphere prevents the leaves from wilting.

• The cutting has no water stress.

• The water flow is cut off before the rooting medium becomes waterlogged.

• Fungus diseases do not appear, the spores that spread them are continually washed away.

• If a soil warming cable is used in conjunction with the mist, the best growing temperature can be maintained.

• Less shading is required which gives the cuttings extra light for growth.

All cuttings root more easily under mist although it is obviously unnecessary for the common, easy to root subjects. The main advantage of mist propagation for the amateur gardener is that it increases the range of plants which can be propagated, especially difficult trees and shrubs.

A mist propagator will increase the humidity of the greenhouse, this could lead to fungus disease problems, especially in autumn. A polythene structure with a fold down front, to contain the unit overcomes this, see Fig 15, page 18.

Weaning

Sudden removal from mist will cause rooted cuttings to collapse. It takes a week or so to accustom the plants to new conditions, this can be done by one of the following ways:

• Reduce the frequency of the mist.

• Place the pots or trays in a very shady place, eg under the staging.

• Place the pots or trays in a large polythene bag and gradually open it up before removing it completely in ten days or so.

Do not pot rooted cuttings up until they have been thoroughly weaned. Cuttings which have been rooted late in the year are best left until spring before potting up. Keep them in a cool part of the greenhouse and give a very light feed.

Seeds

A mist propagator is excellent for germinating very small seeds and some difficult ones such as polyanthus and strawberries. Remove the tray of seedlings from mist as soon as the seeds have germinated.

Note: In hard water districts the electrodes on the electronic leaf may become coated with residues. This is best removed with very fine wet-and-dry abrasive paper.

Difficult to Root Cuttings Which Will Give Over 50 per cent Success Under Mist

Species	*Cutting*	*When to take*	*Wound?**
Acer palmatum	Softwood	May	Yes
Acer davidii	Semi-hardwood	September	Yes
Azaleas (deciduous)	Softwood	April-May	Yes
Betula (birch)	Softwood	May-June	Yes
Camellia	Semi-hardwood	June-July	Yes
Chamaecyparis	Semi-hardwood	September	Yes
Clematis	Softwood	May	No
Cotinus	Softwood	June	No
Garrya	Hardwood	September	No
Leptospernum	Semi-hardwood	July	No
Magnolia	Softwood	May	Yes
Pieris	Semi-hardwood	July	No
Prunus	Softwood	May	Yes
Rhododendron	Semi-hardwood	November	Yes
Wisteria	Side shoots	June	No

* To wound scrape a little bark from one side of the base of the cutting

Hardening Off

The tissues of a greenhouse plant are weaker than those of a similar plant that has been grown outside. Greenhouse plants will suffer a serious check to growth and may possibly die if planted directly outside. This is true for hardy as well as half-hardy species. The process that prepares greenhouse plants for the rigours of outside conditions is called 'hardening off'.

Hardening off is a slow process and takes at least two weeks in late spring, less time in early summer.

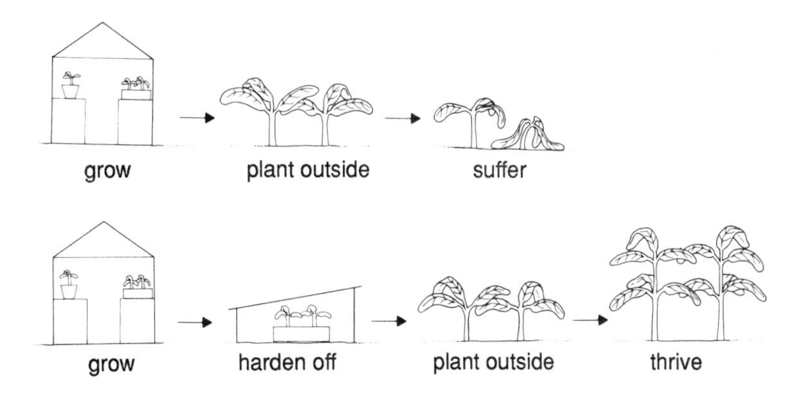

79 Diagram showing the need for hardening off

Hardening Off Greenhouse Plants

1 Transfer the trays of plants to be hardened off into larger trays. The type used for chitting potatoes are ideal as they will stack.

2 Each morning place the trays outside into a position which is sheltered from the wind. Water the plants if necessary.

3 Each evening return the trays to the greenhouse.

4 After a week to ten days, if no frost is forecast, cover with horticultural fleece and leave out overnight.

5 After four more nights remove the fleece.

6 After two or three more days the plants can be transplanted into the garden.

Note: Do not leave the plants outside at night if frost is forecast.

Hardening Off Using a Cold Frame

1 Site the cold frame where it will not receive direct sunlight.

2 Transfer trays and/or pots of plants to a cold frame. When watering plants in a cold frame take care that the plants around the edge of the frame get sufficient water.

3 Give a small amount of ventilation each day and close up at night. If frost is forecast cover the cold frame with a piece of old carpet (or substitute) during the night.

4 Increase the ventilation gradually during the next two weeks until the frame top is completely removed during the day. Give increasing ventilation at night.

5 Two or three days later transfer the plants outside.

Remember: all plants should be thoroughly watered half an hour before planting out in the garden.

4

Growing Flowers

A greenhouse greatly increases the range of flowers which can be grown. If an electric propagator is available and a frost-free area maintained then the range is very large indeed, including bedding plants, plants for the house and conservatory, plants for flower arranging, hardy biennials and perennials, chrysanthemums, dahlias and alpines.

Plants Suitable for Summer Bedding Which Can Be Grown From Seeds

Plant	*Sowing Time*	*Temp* °C	°F	*Germination Time*	*Flowering*
Ageratum	March	18	65	2 weeks	June-September
Alyssum	March	13	55	1/2 weeks	May-September
Antirrhinum	March	18	65	2 weeks	July-September
Aster	March	18	65	2 weeks	August-September
Begonia	February	20	68	3/4 weeks	May-October
Carnation	February	15	60	2/3 weeks	June-October
Dahlia	March	15	60	2 weeks	July-October
Gazania	February	16	62	2/3 weeks	July-September
Geranium*	February	21	70	1/3 weeks	June-October
Impatiens	February	18	65	2/3 weeks	May-October
Lobelia	February	21	70	2/3 weeks	May-October
Marigold African	March	21	70	1/2 weeks	June-October
Marigold French	March/April	21	70	1/2 weeks	June-October
Mesembryanthemum	March	16	62	2 weeks	June-August
Mimulus	March	16	62	2/3 weeks	May-September
Nemesia	March	15	60	2/3 weeks	May-August
Nicotiana	March	18	65	2/3 weeks	June-October
Petunia	March	18	65	2/3 weeks	May-October
Phlox (annual)	March	16	62	2/3 weeks	June-September
Ricinus	March	21	70	3 weeks	foliage plant
Salvia	March	18	65	2/3 weeks	June-Ocotober
Stock	March	18	65	2 weeks	June-September
Tagetes	March	18	65	1/2 weeks	June-October
Verbena	March	20	68	3 weeks	June-October
Zinnia	April	18	65	1/2 weeks	June-September

* Geranium seeds are very expensive, but they need be purchased only once, as new plants can be raised from cuttings in following years.

Bedding Plants

Most summer bedding plants are grown from seeds as described in Chapter 3; use this information, together with the chart, for good results.

Note that the dates quoted in the chart are for the Midlands, most other areas will be somewhat earlier and a few will be a little later. *Do not sow too soon* as later sowings tend to catch up, while too early sowings may become drawn and rootbound.

The temperatures quoted are optimum, a little cooler will increase germination time and a lot cooler may seriously reduce the number of seeds which germinate.

When pricking out bedding plants it is a good idea to pot a few seedlings up into 9cm (3in) pots. They make attractive house plants and even if not used for that purpose are excellent for bedding out, as they are large and have a good root ball so move without a check. Antirrhinum, Dahlia, Gazania, Geranium, Marigolds, Ricinus, Salvia, Tagetes and Zinnias are better grown in pots if space allows. The greenhouse tends to get rather full during April and early May — extra space is easily made available by fitting shelves (Robinsons have an excellent range).

80 Schizanthus

Plants for the House & Conservatory

The greenhouse can be used to provide plants for the house and conservatory in the following ways:

• House plants are grown from seeds in a similar way to bedding plants. They are usually pricked out into 9cm (3in) pots and potted on once into a larger pot, before being taken into the house.

• When existing house plants become overgrow, they can be taken to the greenhouse for propagation by cuttings or division.

• Flowering perennials can be kept in the greenhouse during the time they are not in flower. Tap them from the pot, tease off about half of the compost and replace it with new. This will keep the plant in good condition. Continue to feed the plants in spring and summer, do not feed in winter.

• Spring bulbs* can be grown in individual pots in the greenhouse. Bulb fibre is better than standard composts for this purpose. They will come into flower at least a month earlier than those outside. When the flower buds begin to show, plant four or five bulbs which are at the same stage of growth into a bowl, then all the bulbs in the bowl will then be in flower at the same time.

• Some hardy annuals* when sown in the autumn make colourful pot plants, eg dwarf marigolds. Other hardy annuals will produce spring cut flowers when sown in the greenhouse border in September/October, eg cornflowers and larkspur.

• Greenhouse bulbs* and corms* planted in the autumn for pot plants or cut flowers, eg anemones and ranunculus.

* A cold greenhouse is suitable for these, but do not allow compost in pots to freeze.

Foliage Pot Plants Suitable for Raising in the Amateur's Greenhouse

Plant	*Propagation*	*Notes*
Abutilon	Seeds in spring	Shade in summer, keep in house in winter. Grown for foliage and flowers. Reduce to half size by autumn pruning.
Asparagus fern (plumosus)	Seeds in spring also division	Keep several pots under the greenhouse staging to provide foliage for flower arrangments.
Asparagus (sprengeri)	Seeds in spring	Trails down to floor. Keep out of direct sunlight.
Begonia rex	Leaf cuttings	Little water in winter. Stand on tray of moist pebbles to keep air humid, do not wet the leaves.
Box	Stem cuttings in summer	A good foliage plant which can be clipped to shape. Does not require shade, water well. Hardy.
Spider plant	From runners	Some shade in summer, plenty of water in summer, little in winter.
Coffee plant	Sow unroasted coffee beans	Foliage plant, prune in spring, keep in house in winter, give a little shade and water well.
Coleus	Seeds in March Stem cuttings	Brightly coloured foliage. Pinch out leading shoot to make plant bushy. Pinch off flower stalks as they appear. In hard water areas, use rainwater.
Eucalyptus	Seeds in spring	Attractive trees which make good pot plants, will stand full sun. Plenty of water in summer, little in winter. Cut back to keep a supply of young leaves. Globulus (blue gum), Gunnii (cedar gum) and Citriodora with its lemon scented leaves are easy to grow.
Grevillea and Jacaranda	Seeds in summer	Easy to grow African trees, good foliage plants for two or three years after which time discard them.
Ivy	Stem cuttings	Shade well, keep frost free, do not allow compost to dry out. Better in a humid atmosphere. Pinch tips to keep bushy.
Peperomia	Stem cuttings Leaf cuttings of plants without stems	Good light required but not direct sun. Allow compost to dry between waterings. Keep in a small pot.
Pelargoniums (geraniums)	Stem cuttings	Good light but not direct midday sun. Average water in summer, very little in winter. Leaves also scented.

Flowering Pot Plants Suitable for Raising in the Amateur's Greenhouse		
Plant	*Propagation*	*Notes*
Achimenes	Tubers in March	Water with tepid water, support with twigs.
Begonia	Seeds in spring Cuttings	Many different types. Water when beginning to dry out, keep atmosphere humid. Give some shade.
Capsicum	Seeds in March	An annual grown for its attractive fruit.
Cyclamen	Seeds in April	Flowers in January.
Exacum	Seeds in March	Blue sweetly scented annual, prick out five plants into a 9cm (3½in) pot.
Fuchsia	Seeds in April	Perennial, will flower from July-October.
Freesia	Seeds in March Bulbs	Soak in warm water for 24 hours.
Gardenia	Seeds in early spring	Heavily scented flowers. Keep in a 15cm (6in) pot.
Geranium	Seeds in February Cuttings in August	Allow cutting to dry for 24 hours before inserting. No rooting powder needed.
Gerbera	Seeds in March	Striking flowers on long stems, rather difficult to grow.
Gloxinia	Seeds in February or tubers in March	Must be shaded, Feed as flowers form, dry off after flowering.
Impatiens	Seeds in March	Busy Lizzi, easy to grow but subject to aphids
Lantana	Seeds in spring Cuttings	Flowers all year
Pansy	Seeds January to September	Very versatile plant which will flower from February until October.
Plumbago	Seeds in April	Excellent flowering perennial for the conservatory.
Polyanthus and primrose	Seeds March-August	Flowers December-June. Grow *cool* and water regularly.
Saintpaulia	Seeds in March Leaf cuttings	Do not cover seeds. Requires fairly dense shade
Salpiglossis	Seeds in March	Superb pot plant, flowers from July to September. Pinch out main stem to give a bushy plant.
Stephanotis	Seeds in early spring	Climber. Flowers heavily scented
Streptocarpus	Seeds in March	Shade and grow cool. Remove old flower stems. Will flower for several years, keep rather dry in winter.

Hardy Plants Suitable for Raising in the Amateur's Greenhouse		
Plant	*Sowing time*	*Notes*
Aquilegia	May	Try Mckana's Hybrids and Dragonfly Hybrids.
Arabis	June	Suitable for rockery or alpine garden.
Armeria (Thrift)	May	Suitable for rockery, alpine or front of border.
Bellis (Daisy)	June-July	Excellent for spring bedding. Long flowering period. Large double flowers and miniatures available.
Campanula (Canterbury Bells)	May	Biennial for early summer bedding; Cup and saucer varieties are more colourful.
Coreopsis	April	A good border plant which also provides cut flowers.
Dianthus	June	Buy the perennial type; a colourful rock plant.
Digitalis (Foxglove)	June	Biennial, good for early summer display. Many colourful hybrids available. Tolerates shade.
Doronicum	May	Gives a good show of yellow flowers in April/May.
Gaillardia (Blanket flower)	April	Requires sunny position and may need staking.
Gypsophila (Babies' breath)	April	Good middle border plant which is traditionally cut to display with sweet peas.
Hollyhock	May	Very tall cottage garden plant. Subject to fungus disease, spray with Murphy systemic action fungicide.
Lavender	April	Makes an attractive hedge, cut flowers early for drying.
Edelweiss	April	An interesting and long flowering rock plant.
Lupin	May	Pot on in 22cm (9in) pots, may flower first year.
Lychnis	May	Alpine and tall, border types available.
Forget-me-not	May	Biennial, excellent for spring bedding. Buy a compact variety.
Pansy	up until September	Only sow winter hardy varieties after May.
Polyanthus	up until August	Very versatile — good for pots, cutting and bedding.
Primula	April	Germinate in cool conditions. Best to collect own seed as soon as ripe and sow immediately.
Brompton stock	June	Good pot plant. Not fully hardy, in cold areas plant out after worst of the winter is over. Fragrant.
Sweet William	May	Good border plant; also suitable for cutting
Verbascum	May	Biennial — a striking plant often grown in wildlife gardens.
Veronica	May	Rock garden plant with an irregular saucer shaped flower.

Hardy Biennials & Perennials

When the bedding plants and vegetables are hardening-off in May, propagator and bench space become available. A good way of using this space is to raise hardy biennials and hardy perennials from seeds. Sow, germinate and prick out into individual pots. Grow on in the greenhouse and plant out in the flowering positions when space is available. These plants will flower the following year; after which pull up the biennials and leave the perennials to flower in subsequent years.

Hundreds of species of plants are grown in this way, the chart opposite contains popular ones which the author has found to be particularly successful, and are perennials unless stated otherwise.

Hanging Baskets

The greenhouse can be used for hanging basket production in three ways:

- Keeping suitable plants from one year to the next for propagation (the greenhouse must have a frost-free area).
- Propagate plants for hanging baskets from seeds and cuttings.
- Growing on after the baskets have been planted up. This enables mature baskets to be positioned as soon as the weather is suitable.

All the plants in the photograph were raised in an unheated Robinsons greenhouse equipped with a home-made propagator. The propagator provided a frost-free area for the perennials in very cold weather. Cuttings were taken in February and seeds were sown during March and April. The secret of a good hanging basket is to have the largest one possible. Small hanging baskets are more difficult to keep watered than large ones. Moisture retaining agents are available for mixing with hanging basket composts (eg Chempak Supergel). These increase the water capacity of the basket but they make no difference to the amount of water the plants use.

Note that hanging baskets use a lot of water and need daily attention, they may even need watering on wet days. The best way to check for water is to test the weight of the basket, by lifting from underneath.

81 Plants for hanging baskets propagated in a greenhouse will flower earlier. These flowers were photographed in the Midlands at the end of May

Raising Hanging Basket Plants

Cuttings of trailing half-hardy perennials are

best taken from the baskets in August or September, by May however they have usually grown too large. A good way of overcoming this is to take the cuttings, grow them on and keep through the winter. In February take cuttings from the new plants and these will be an ideal size when required in May.

Helichrysum petiolare and *Plecthranthus australus* (Swedish ivy) are ideal for this purpose.

Take geranium cuttings in August, allow them to dry for 24 hours before inserting in the rooting medium. Pot up individually and winter in a frost-free area, water very sparingly.

Surfinia — the perennial petunia — is an excellent hanging basket plant; take off some long stems in late August, cut into 5cm (2in) lengths and root them in the propagator. Keep frost free during the winter.

Tuberous rooted begonias are widely used in hanging baskets. At the end of the season, lift the tubers from the basket, brush off the compost and allow the plant to die down. Dust the tubers with a little sulphur, pack them in dry peat and store, in a cool frost-proof place. In February transfer them to a warm room. Inspect the tubers regularly and when shoots begin to appear, pot up in a soilless multipurpose compost, shoots uppermost and cover with 2cm (1in) of compost. Grow on in the propagator and transfer to the staging when conditions are warm enough.

Planting a Hanging Basket

1. Obtain the largest suitable basket and decide whether it is to be viewed from one side only, or from all sides. (One sided ones are not planted up at the back.)
2. Stand the basket on a 22cm (9in) pot.
3. Line the bottom half of the basket with moss. If a complete liner is being used instead of moss cut it in such a way that trailing plants can be set, half way up the basket.
4. Cut a circle of plastic, half the diameter of the basket and place it in the bottom to form a well. Puncture the centre of the well with one small hole.
5. Half fill the basket with a good general purpose compost (not John Innes as it is too heavy).
6. Place the recommended number of Osmocote* (or similar) tablets on the top.
7. Plant up a number of trailing plants by feeding the plants through the side and putting the roots into the compost.
8. Line the top half of the basket.
9. Add a little more compost.
10. Take the larger, pot grown plants, remove the pots and arrange them on the compost with the soil level about one centimetre (half an inch) below the top of the basket.
11. Fill the spaces between the pots with compost, firming it gently to avoid leaving any empty space.
12. Plant a few more trailing plants around the edge, allowing them to overhang the side.
13. Cover the surface of the compost with moss.
14. Water well.
15. Care for in the greenhouse until weather conditions allow hanging out.

* Osmocote tablets contain a slow release fertiliser and remove the need to feed.

Hanging Basket Plants Which are Grown From Seed				
		Germination		
		Temp		*Time*
Plant	*Sowing Date*	*°C*	*°F*	
Alyssum	March	13	55	2 weeks
Begonia	February	20	68	3/4 weeks
Brachycome (Swan river daisy)	April	18	65	2 weeks
Campanula fragilis	March	15	60	3/4 weeks
Erigeron profusion	March	15	60	3/4 weeks
Geranium	January (cuttings also)	21	70	1/3 weeks
Impatiens (Busy Lizzi)	February	18	65	2/3 weeks
Lobelia (trailing)	February	21	70	2/3 weeks
Marigold	March	21	70	1/2 weeks
Nasturtium	March	15	60	3/4 weeks
Nolana	March	15	60	2 weeks
Petunia	March	18	65	2/3 weeks
Sanvitalia (Creeping zinnia)	March	15	60	3/4 weeks
Tagetes	March	18	65	1/2 weeks
Verbena	March	20	68	3 weeks

Plants for Flower Arrangers

The greenhouse can be used to increase the range of material available to flower arrangers, and a few ideas are listed below:

• Keep a few pots of *Asparagus plumosus* on the floor just underneath the staging. This is a useful source of greenery all the year round. It is a perennial and very easy to grow from seeds.

• Grow a pittosporum (a privet-like shrub with wavy edged leaves) in a large pot and move it into the greenhouse during the winter months.

• Raise the everlasting hardy annuals Acroclinium, Ammobium, Rhodanthe, *Scabious stellata* and Xeranthemum in a similar way to bedding plants and plant outside in rows for cutting.

• Sow the half-hardy everlasting flowers Carthamus, Craspedia, Helichrysum and Statice in late March. Prick these out into individual pots, grow on, harden off and plant outside. Harvest before the flowers are fully open and hang upside-down to dry.

• Raise the perennial *Statice dumosa* from seed in the greenhouse and plant outside. The seed heads will dry and last throughout the winter.

• Grow Bells of Ireland from seeds and prick out into 9cm (4in) pots. Stop watering when the flower spikes are 25cm (10in) long, and move them to a dry atmosphere. As the plants dry out, they will become straw like, both in colour and texture. Alternatively, cut the flower spikes, with the longest possible stems, and stand in 10cm (4in) of a mixture of two parts water and one part glycerine, to which a systemic fungicide (eg Benlate or Nimrod T) has been added. Keep in a dark, dry place and the flowers will absorb the glycerine in two weeks or so. The flower spikes will be an attractive golden yel-

82 Growing Asparagus plumosus for flower arranging in pots under the greenhouse staging

83 (below left) Bells of Ireland — on the left is a growing plant, on the right preserved with glycerine (in a pot just for the photograph)

84 (below right) These grasses grew from seed in only eight weeks, they should be cut and dried just before the flowers open

low and will keep in good condition for well over a year. Note: when mixing glycerine with water the water must be very hot, allow it to cool before use.

• Purchase *Arum calla* rhizomes from a bulb merchant and grow in 22 cm (9 inch) pots. These can be kept on the floor of the greenhouse just underneath the staging. They require plenty of water — even in winter when they die back. In very frosty weather, cover them over with some insulating material.

Fuchsias

Most fuchsias are half hardy and need to be kept frost free during the winter. The fuchsia in the photograph overleaf, seen here on the first day of July, was grown in a frost-free (but otherwise unheated) greenhouse from a cutting taken in March.

Growing Standard Fuschias

1. Begin to water over-wintered fuchsias as soon as temperatures begin to rise. In the Midlands this is usually in March.
2. Take cuttings from the new growth as soon as it is large enough.
3. Root the cuttings in a propagator.
4. Pot up rooted cuttings in 7cm (3in) pots of multi-purpose compost.
5. As side shoots develop, rub them out.
6. Pot on into a 10 cm (4in) pot.
7. Push a thin cane vertically to the bottom of the pot, as near to the base of the plant as possible.
8. Tie the main stem to the cane as necessary.
9. Feed and water regularly and remove all side shoots as they appear.
10. Pot on to a larger pot a 12 or 15cm (5 or 6in).
11. When the plant is at the required height, stop removing side shoots at the top and the plant will then form a head.
12. Harden off and plant out.

85 Standard fuchsia raised in the greenhouse

Chrysanthemums

Chrysanthemums have been cultivated in China since before 500BC. They were introduced into Britain at the end of the eighteenth century and are second only to roses in their commercial importance.

There are several different species of chrysanthemums, some are annuals and used as bedding plants. The one described here is the half-hardy perennial which is used to produce cut flowers. Chrysanthemums will survive some frost and are a good subject for an unheated greenhouse, especially as they are kept outside during the summer months allowing the greenhouse to be used for other purposes.

There are several different shapes of chrysanthemum flowers and many different colours. The important difference as far as the grower is concerned, is between spray chrysanthemums and the large individual blooms. The latter take more time but, apart from disbudding, they are grown in the same way.

The instructions in the chart are for varieties that will flower from September to November and are suitable for the unheated greenhouse.

Growing Chrysanthemums as Cut Flowers

Getting Started

1. Consult specialist catalogues, decide which varieties you wish to grow and order a number of rooted cuttings to arrive in the spring.
2. Pot up the cuttings in 9cm (3.5in) pots filled with a good potting compost.
3. Place on the greenhouse staging and when the plant has six full-sized leaves, pinch out the top. This is known as 'stopping'. Stopping induces the lower buds to grow and as a result there are several main shoots instead of just one.
4. When the roots fill the compost, pot on into a 13cm (5in) pot.
5. Feed regularly according to the compost manufacturer's instructions.
6. Harden off when the weather permits and keep the plants outside.

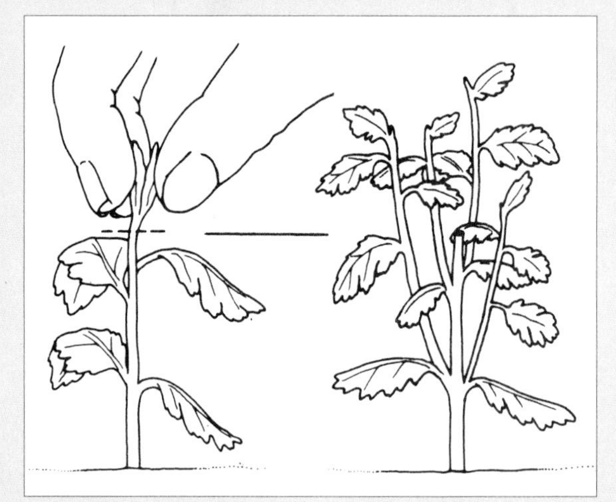

86 Stopping encourages several main shoots instead of just one

Outside Work

1. Pot up into 23cm (9inch) pots. A home-made soil based compost with plenty of fibrous material and John Innes base added at the number 3 rate. Firm the compost hard around the outside edges of the pot, using a short length of wood the thickness of a broom handle.
2. Stake each plant with a 1.4 metre (4ft) cane and tie each stem to it; or stake with four canes and tie strings around the canes.
3. Place the pots in a line and tie the canes to a horizontal wire that is stretched between two posts for this purpose.
4. Water as required and feed each week with a fertiliser, diluted according to the manufacturer's instructions.

Recipe for a home-made feed:

150 g (5 oz) of potassium nitrate

60 g (2 oz) of ammonium nitrate

Dissolve in one litre (1.75 pints) of water. Dilute the solution 300 times, that is 3ml in one litre (1 fl oz in 15 pints) and water the chrysanthemums with it once a week.

Earlier flowering varieties should be left to bloom outside and later flowering ones will require some heat. A recent practice is to transfer late flowerers from the greenhouse to the conservatory when temperatures become low.

Note that the stock may become diseased as years go by, so to avoid this purchase new cuttings every third or fourth year.

5 For **blooms**: As the sideshoots develop break them off but leave the buds at the top of the stem. When the top group of buds are large enough to handle, remove all of them except the terminal bud — this will become the flower. The purpose of this is to produce a large flower with a long stem.

For **sprays**: Remove the terminal bud when it is large enough to handle. The purpose of this is to have a group of flowers on a single stem, open at the same time.

6 Before taking them inside the greenhouse, spray with a systemic insecticide and a systemic fungicide. (Organic growers will of course omit this.)

Flowering

1 The actual timing of the move into the greenhouse will vary according to district, the aim is to avoid any frost on the flower buds. Carry the plants into the greenhouse *pot first*. Line them up leaving 45cm (18in) either way between the pots.
2 Give maximum ventilation, only closing at night when frost is forecast.
3 Continue to water and feed.
4 Cut the blooms complete with a long stem, when the outside petals are spread and the inside ones still in a tight cluster.
5 Gently smash the bottom 3cm (1in) of the stem with a hammer.
6 Stand the flowers in a bucket of water overnight. The water should almost (but not quite) reach the blooms. This 'conditioning' increases the life of the flowers when taken indoors.
7 After cutting all the flowers, discard any plants that show signs of weakness or disease.

Preserving the Stock.

1 Cut off any regrowth from the remaining plants and place them in a sheltered position outside the greenhouse.
2 Leave the plants outside until there has been a week's cold weather when temperatures have not risen above 5°C (40°F).
3 After this treatment remove all the dead leaves and place the plants under the greenhouse staging. During periods of intense cold it may be necessary to give some protection to prevent the compost in the pots from freezing.
4 In late January remove the stools into frost free conditions and give a *little* water.
5 As spring sunshine increases temperatures and new shoots appear, increase the watering but do not feed.
6 When the shoots are large enough take cuttings, in most districts this will be during March and April.
7 Discard the stools.

The pot chrysanthemums which are sold all the year round have been grown in light-controlled conditions. They have also been treated with a substance which prevents them from growing to their full height of several feet. Do not be tempted to propagate from these as disappointment will result. They should be discarded after they have finished flowering.

87 Autumn chrysanthemums following a crop of tomatoes in an unheated greenhouse

88 Pot chrysanthemums staked to prevent wind damage

89 Taking a chrysanthemum cutting

Chrysanthemum Trouble Shooter			
Symptoms	*Cause*	*Treatment*	*Prevention*
Cutting or plant wilts. Roots appear black and rotted.	Fungus	Remove infected plants. Drench soil with Benomyl.	Use sterile growing medium. Water with tap water.
Petals become water-soaked. Mouldy patches in flowers.	Grey mould	A little late, but try a fungicide spray.	Increase ventilation. Remove diseased material. Do not grow badly affected varieties.
Powdery white growth on leaves.	Powdery mildew	Spray with fungicide.	Remove infected leaves. Keep plants properly watered.
Lower leaves turn yellow then brown, progresses up plant. Bark peels at base.	Wilt (a fungus)	Remove infected plants, apply Benomyl to compost of healthy plants.	Use sterilised compost. Take cuttings from healthy stock only.

Dahlias

There are two ways of using the greenhouse to grow this popular half-hardy perennial. For both methods the soil where they are to be grown should be well prepared and manured. Dahlias thrive best in a soil which is high in nutrients and is moisture retentive.

- Pot up tubers in February in 22cm (9 inch) pots, grow on, harden off and plant out when the danger of frost is over. This method gives early flowers and a long display.
- Propagate new plants by cuttings. This method does not give such early flowers but the flowers are larger and better than those grown by the first method.

Note that the plants from which the cuttings were taken can also be planted up in the garden. Discard these at the end of the season and lift and store the tubers from the new cuttings.

90 Dahlias flowering in July from a cutting taken in March

91 Dahlia and chrysanthemum grown under the staging, now ready for taking cuttings

Growing Dahlias

1 At the end of the growing season, cut the dahlias off at ground level.

2 Dig up the tubers, tease off as much soil as possible and place them on the greenhouse staging *upsidedown* to dry off.

3 When dry, remove any remaining soil and dust the tubers with sulphur.

4 Pack in a box of dry peat, and store in a dry, frost-free shed.

5 In February, remove the tubers and pot them up in 22cm (9in) pots. (The tubers may be divided up, but *there must be a piece of stem* attached to each tuber otherwise it will not grow.

6 If bench space is short put the pots underneath the staging. Water.

7 As the season warms up the tubers will begin to grow — this may take quite a long time.

8 As the shoots become large enough take and strike cuttings. (See Chapter 3.)

9 Pot up rooted cuttings in 13cm (5in) pots filled with a good potting compost. These must of course be on the staging in good light.

10 Grow on and harden off at the appropriate time.

Sweet Peas

Sweet peas can be produced early in the season from plants raised in the greenhouse. Although September sowing is often recommended, the author finds that sowing as early as this produces unwieldy plants long before the weather allows planting outside in the garden. If space is available in the border of a cold greenhouse then a September sowing will produce excellent, long-stemmed flowers from late April onwards.

Growing Sweet Peas

1. In late October fill 7cm (3in) pots with a multipurpose compost. (Washing-up liquid containers, with the tops and bottoms sliced off, are better. Stand in a tray and tie a piece of string around to stop them falling over. When planting out, the container is planted as well.)
2. Sow one sweet pea in each by pushing it into the compost to a depth of 2cm (1in). Save any unused seeds. Water and leave to germinate.
3. When the plants have four leaves, pinch out the top. This is very important as the side shoots which then grow are much stronger than the leader.
4. During cold spells cover the plants with fleece and leave it on day and night. The sweet pea plant is fairly hardy and can stand a little frost; do not allow the compost to freeze (page 13).
5. Harden off about a month or so before bedding plants.
6. Plant out against supports. Alongside each plant sow an unused seed. These will grow and 'take over' as the older plants finish flowering.

Alpines

Alpine plants are generally frost hardy, but they may die during British winters from damp conditions. A cold greenhouse with *good ventilation* gives alpines the best possible conditions in a British winter. The greenhouse, or a sealed off section, is best entirely devoted to alpines. It is damp rather than cold that kills many alpine plants. The top ventilators should be open all the time, the side ventilators should be open on the leeward and closed on the windward side.

In late spring the plants can be moved outside, without the hardening off process. If they are kept inside during the summer then shading is essential from April onwards.

Small conifers, small flowered spring bulbs, low growing rock plants, primulas, lewisias and very many other types may be included in a display. Readers are advised to consult the Alpine Society who will put them in touch with a local enthusiast.

Growing Alpines

1. Select shallow pots of either clay or plastic.
2. Mix a John Innes potting compost with double the amount of grit; **or** mix one third grit into a multipurpose soilless compost; **or** mix a compost of equal parts of loam, leaf mould and coarse sand. (For plants that require acid conditions: omit the lime in the John Innes compost; use ericaceous instead of multipurpose compost in the second and use ericaceous instead of leaf mould in the last.)
3. Put a little gravel, or pieces of broken clay pots — concave side — down in the bottom of the pots.
4. Fill with the compost mix and plant.
5. Cover the surface of the compost with a layer of coloured stone chips.
6. Water sparingly.
7. Tier the greenhouse benches and cover with shingle.
8. Display the alpines on or plunged into the shingle.

5

Producing Food

While many food crops can be grown by sowing seeds directly outside, there are considerable advantages in starting crops off in the greenhouse and transferring them outside. A greenhouse can be used to provide salads, fruit and vegetables in two ways:

- Crops grown to maturity in the greenhouse.
- Crop plants are raised in the greenhouse and transferred outside to complete their growth.

92 *Sweetcorn and runner beans grown in root trainers, ready to harden off*

Advantages of raising crop plants in a greenhouse are:

- The crop is unaffected by weather in its early stages of growth.
- Crops are produced early in the season — often when prices are high.
- The growing season is lengthened, this gives a bigger crop and sometimes an extra crop
- Two crops can be grown on the same area by intercropping, for example lettuce plants can be placed between a double row of runner beans.
- Some pests are controlled as the crops are ready for harvest before pests arrive, eg very early broad beans are unlikely to get blackfly.
- The plants go into the garden with strong, healthy root systems and are less likely to suffer from disease.
- Weed control is easier, the need to handweed seedlings is removed and the plants are large enough to compete with new weeds as they appear.
- Sowing is not delayed by bad weather.

Do not forget that the plant varieties mentioned here may be superseded, as new varieties of plants are always being developed. A good source of information about plant varieties is the current seed catalogues.

Lettuce & Salads

Lettuce

The choice of lettuce varieties is of extreme importance; varieties that are suitable for growing in the greenhouse during the winter are quite useless as summer lettuce and visa-versa. Lettuce is fairly hardy and hearted ones can be harvested in the greenhouse as late as December and as early as April.

Lettuce plants raised in the greenhouse and transplanted outside produce a much earlier

93 Different varieties of lettuce in the greenhouse border give a continuity of supply

94 Nine-section trays of lettuce (left) and beetroot plants (right), ready for planting out. Three of each have been removed from the sections

crop than would otherwise be possible. Summer lettuces are best grown entirely outside. After harvesting, a lettuce should be cooled in the refrigerator for half an hour, then put into a polythene bag and stored in the refrigerator until required.

Varieties that stand through the winter for very early spring crops must be given plenty of space and very little water. Increase watering and begin to feed as the temperature increases with early spring sunshine.

Currently the best winter variety of crisp lettuce for the cold greenhouse is Kellys. Sowings in November will produce hearted lettuce by April. There is a wider choice of butterhead (soft) lettuces. Kwiek can be sown in late August and September to give a crop around Christmas time. Debby can be sown from January to crop from early May. If leaves, rather than hearts are wanted, the loose-leaved variety Novita can be sown from September through to mid-February.

Lettuces for harvesting in late summer and early autumn are best grown entirely outside.

Beetroot

Beetroot will stand a little frost and is an ideal crop for early production in a cold greenhouse.

The only real problem is that of 'bolting' (running to seed before forming a beetroot), but that has been largely overcome by plant breeding. Sow beetroot in the greenhouse at least six weeks before the first outside sowings. For transplanting outside further sowings can be made in a similar way to those described for early beetroot (page 73).

Onions

Large Onions — Large onions need a long growing season, varieties such as Kelsae or Mammoth need to be sown in January if weights of 2kg (5lb) are to be reached. Germinate them in a propagator at 16°C (60°F), prick out into individual pots and grow on until planting out time in April.

Salad Onions — This crop is hardy and is easily grown to maturity in a cold greenhouse.

Varieties of Lettuce to Grow in the Greenhouse:			
Variety	*Sowing Dates*	*Harvest Dates*	*Notes*
Kellys	November/December	April/May	Crisp
Debby	January/February	April/May	Butterhead
Kwiek	August/October	November/December	Butterhead
Novita	September/January	November/April	Harvest leaves
Any summer lettuce	February/April	May/July	Transplanted outside

Growing Lettuce

1 Fill 7cm (3in) pots or divided trays with seed compost and water it.
2 Sow two seeds in each pot or section and save the unused seed as it will keep for up to three years.
3 Germinate at a temperature of *less than* 24°C (75°F). Pull out any surplus seedlings leaving one in each pot.
4 When the compost ball is filled with roots and *before* they begin to curl around the bottom of the container, *either* harden off for transplanting outside.
or
5 Plant up in a soil bed at the spacing recommended for the variety. Old growbags may be used instead, the ones in which tomatoes have grown are ideal, add a little more compost and water with a complete fertiliser. Plant six lettuces in each bag. (Do not use the bags for a third time.)
6 Water regularly but take extreme care not to get the soil too wet.
7 Feed weekly with a complete fertiliser that is high in nitrogen, for example Chempak Formula 2.
8 Pull out weeds as they appear.
9 As the lettuces heart up, harvest them by cutting off at ground level with a sharp knife.

American or Land Cress
This salad crop is very similar in appearance and taste to watercress. It is very easy to grow in a cold greenhouse and makes a useful salad crop early in the year.

Radish
Cool conditions are required for the successful production of radish and it should only be grown as a greenhouse crop in late winter and early spring. Select a variety like Cherry Belle or French Breakfast, avoid the long varieties like Icicle and the Spanish ones.

Grow radish in a similar way as described for American Cress *or* grow them in a general purpose compost in a 15cm (6in) pot and about twenty, evenly spaced seeds.

Mustard & Cress
When purchased from a supermarket, this salad usually consists of rape seedlings with a small amount of mustard and cress mixed in. Rape seedlings are very bland, home-grown mustard and cress has a much stronger flavour as there are no rape seedlings.

Mustard and cress can be grown at any time

Growing Early Beetroot

1 Select an early *bolt resistant* variety, Boltardy is a good one, but there are others.
2 Sow three seeds* in each section of a divided tray using a seed compost.
3 Germinate in a propagator.
4 Beetroot seeds are actually clusters of seeds and more than three seedlings should appear in each section. Pull out the weakest seedlings leaving between three and six plants in each.
5 Transfer the trays to the greenhouse bench in good light.
6 Give a weak general purpose feed each week.
7 Prepare a soil bed and rake in a *little* Growmore or other general purpose fertiliser.
8 When there are enough roots to hold the compost into a ball, gently remove the clumps of beetroot from the trays. Do not separate the plants nor disturb the ball of roots.
9 Plant the clumps of beetroot plants in a line with 15cm (6in) between each clump.
10 Water as necessary, pull up weeds as they appear. Further feeding is unnecessary.
11 As the roots become big enough to eat, harvest the larger ones by gently rotating them between the fingers and thumb, this will free them without disturbing the others which are left to grow.
12 Remove the tops by twisting them off.
* Some beetroot seeds are now supplied as 'monogerm', ie each seed produces only one plant, if this type is being used, sow six seeds per segment.

Growing Salad Onions

1 During September remove the remains of the summer crop from a soil bed.
2 Fork over the bed and tread it firm.
3 Rake to a fine tilth.
4 Draw a number of trenches, 1cm (½in) deep and 75cm (3in) wide, 15cm (6in) apart.
5 Use a rose can to thoroughly wet the bottom of each trench.
6 Sprinkle thinly and evenly, seeds of a *winter hardy* variety. Ordinary White Lisbon may not succeed, the seeds must be *Winter Hardy* White Lisbon.
7 Cover the seeds lightly by raking a little soil over them.
8 Keep them moist, but not wet throughout the winter.
9 In early spring begin a weekly feed with a balanced plant food.
10 Remove any weeds that appear.
11 Pull the largest onions as required, leaving the others to grow.

of the year, when temperatures are low a propagator will be required.

These seeds are sown more thickly than is usual for other types, as a result the seedlings tend to lift the compost instead of growing through it. Sow mustard or cress seeds onto five thicknesses of wet kitchen towel on a capillary bed — or sow in a Continental pot of moist seed compost. Do not cover the seeds. Stand the pot in a shallow tray of water.

Growing Land Cress

1 In January or February, prepare a soil bed and rake it to a fine tilth.
2 Make drills 1-2cm (½-1in) deep and 15cm (6in) apart.
3 Water the bottom of each drill and sow thinly (about three per centimetre [½in]).
4 Cover the seeds lightly by raking the excess soil back into the drills.
5 Water and keep weed-free, when the plants are growing strongly add a little nitrogen fertiliser to the water each week.
6 Harvest by removing the larger leaves from the plant at soil level and leave the smaller ones to grow.

Tomatoes

The tomato is a native of South America and is the most widely grown greenhouse crop in Britain. The fruit is of course edible, but all other parts of the plant are poisonous.

Varieties

There are many varieties with various fruit shapes and colours — varieties with very large fruit are most suitable for cooking, while those with very small fruit are said to have the sweetest flavour. The seeds of F1 Hybrid varieties are more expensive than the other types, but they are very reliable and generally worth the extra money.

Raising Tomato Plants

1 Good light is required — do not begin until mid February at the earliest.
2 Fill 9cm (3in) pots with seed compost, water and allow to drain.
3 Sow *one* seed in the centre of each pot by pushing it to a depth of 5mm (¼in) with a cocktail stick.
4 Germinate in a propagator set at 25°C (75°F), this takes less than a week.
5 Reduce the temperature to 20°C (68°F) and leave the plants in the propagator. In warm weather the propagator top can be removed in the daytime to give extra light.
6 As the plants grow, move them apart and do not allow them to touch.
7 Begin feeding according to the instructions on the bag of compost and feed each week. (The amount of plant nutrients in a compost varies according to its type.)
8 As soon as the plants reach the top of the propagator, move them into the lightest part of the greenhouse. In cold weather, cover at night with horticultural fleece.
9 Check the roots now and again by tapping a plant from its pot, when they appear at the surface of the ball, pot on into potting or general purpose compost in 13cm (5in) pots.
10 Grow on, feeding regularly and moving apart as necessary, until the first flowers appear.
11 When two or three flowers are fully opened plant up into the fruiting positions.

Note that extra plants can be obtained by using side shoots as cuttings — they root very quickly.

Tomato Plant Trouble Shooter

Symptoms	*Probable cause*	*Possible cause*
Leaves look dark blue; growth hard	Temperature too low	Plants in a draught
Plants very pale green	Not enough light	Temperature too high
Lower leaves yellow, poor growth	Waterlogged	
Curled leaves with shrivelled edges. Very dark green	Overfeeding	
Plants tall and spindly	Pots too close together	Not enough ventilation

Problems Caused by Chemical Deficiency in Tomatoes

Symptoms	*Chemical Deficient*
A black patch at the flower end of the fruit — 'blossom end rot'	*Calcium
Poor growth and irregular yellow/brown patches between the leaf veins of the older leaves	Magnesium
New leaves are pale green, small and the stems are thin	Nitrogen
Blotchy ripening, an area of green by the stalk of a red fruit. Misshapen and hollow fruit.	Potassium (potash)

* This is usually caused by faulty watering. There may be enough calcium in the compost but dry conditions prevent the plant from absorbing it.

Purchasing Plants.
If no propagator or other form of heat is available, tomato plants should be purchased at the beginning of May (for the Midlands, earlier in other areas). The best plants are fairly dark green and short jointed, plants that are standing outside shops should be avoided as they are probably receiving a 'check'. If a propagator is available, good quality tomato plants are easily raised from seeds.

Tomato Feeds
Correct feeding will keep tomato plants healthy and double or triple the yield of fruit. Tomato feeds are available as liquid concentrates and soluble powders. Most powders are cheaper to use than liquids and are just as good. It is very important that the manufacturers' instructions

95 Tomatoes with blossom end rot

Growing Tomatoes — Operations Common to All Methods of Production

Training

An untrained plant grows into a low spreading bush which is unsuitable for greenhouse production. It takes up too large an area and the space above it is wasted. To overcome this, tomato plants are trained as single stems.

- Identify the sideshoots.
- When a sideshoot is about 5cm (2in) long, hold it between the finger and the thumb and apply a little sidewards pressure. The sideshoot will snap off, leaving the leaf below intact.
- Repeat this operation as necessary during the growing season.

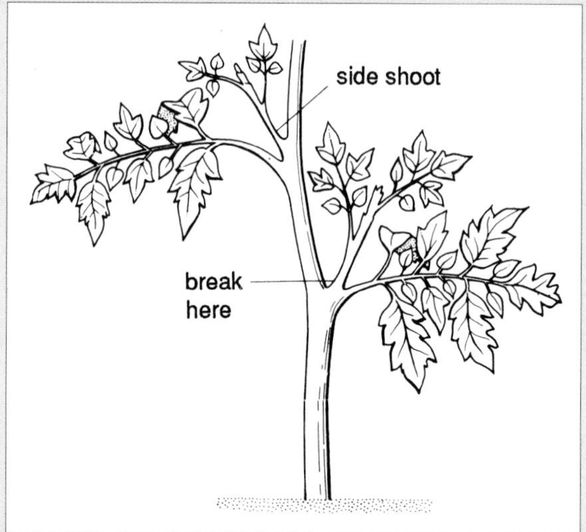

96 Side shoot removal

Support

- Tie a length of tomato twine (or nylon string) *loosely*, with a knot that will not slip, around the stem, 15cm (6in) or so from soil level.
- Hold the twine above the plant and turn it around the stem once or twice.
- Fix the string to a firm support above the plant. (Robinsons of Winchester supply a strong aluminium bracket which is bolted into the roof glazing bars to hold the plant supports.)
- As the plant grows, give the string an occasional twist around the stem.

Lowering the Plants

This enables extra trusses to be grown on each plant, the actual number which each plant produces depends upon the area and the season.

- When the tops of the plants have reached the glass, do not pinch them out but untie the supporting string and tie another length on to it. Lower the plant, by laying the stem on the floor until the lowest fruit is 15cm (6in) from the ground.
- Tie the string to a new support and allow the plant to continue its upward growth.
- If space does not allow the plants to be lowered in the way described, train them along the underside of the greenhouse roof.

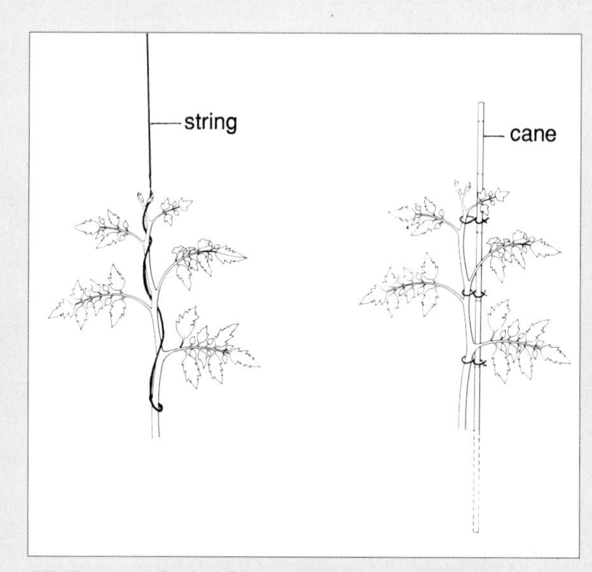

97 Two methods of supporting tomato plants

By using one of these methods it is possible to get up to twenty trusses on one plant in a cold greenhouse in the Midlands.

An Alternate Support

- Push a clean garden cane upright into the soil, alongside the stem and about 5cm (2 inches) from the base.
- Tie the stem to the cane every 25 cm (10 inches) or so. Make sure that the string is tied tightly to the cane and loosely around the stem.

Watering

In hot weather large tomato plants can use up to 2 litres (3.5 pints) of water each day. It is important to keep the compost wet, but not waterlogged.

- Check each day and water as necessary. (See chapter 3.)
- Direct a jet of water directly into the flowers. This is very important as it assists pollination and fruit set.
- In early autumn, when the days are shorter and cooler, water the compost but keep the foliage dry.
- Each week add tomato feed to the water; observe the growing points of the plants and if they show signs of reduced vigour increase the feeding to twice a week. This will give better results than giving extra feed once a week.

Lower Leaves

Lower leaf removal increases the air circulation and helps to prevent fungus diseases.

- When the first fruit is picked, cut off the leaves below the first truss with a sharp knife.
- Continue to remove the leaves progressively from the bottom. Do *not* take any leaves that are *above* the ripening trusses, unless they are diseased.

Ventilation

- In hot weather, if automatic ventilators are not fitted, leave all the ventilators fully open while you are away. Too little ventilation is much more harmful than too much.
- When temperatures fall below 17°C (64°F) reduce ventilation.
- Leave at least one ventilator open on damp autumn days as a fungus control measure.

Harvesting

- Harvest when the fruit is turning colour but is still firm and not fully ripe.
- Remove each fruit, complete with calyx, by lifting upwards and snapping the stem.
- Take the fruit indoors immediately as hot sun will cause it to lose condition.
- At the end of the season any unripe trusses should be removed whole and hung up in a frost-free shed. The fruit will continue to ripen and will be perfectly good to eat.

Removing Tomato Plants

At the end of the season old tomato plants, together with their roots should be removed as soon as possible. The discarded material should be properly composted, well away from the greenhouse.

Tomato Trouble Shooter (Mature Plants)

Symptoms	*Cause*	*Treatment*	*Prevention*
Older leaves curl upwards	Large day/night temperature difference		
Holes in leaves, stems & fruit	Tomato moth caterpillars	Hand pick. Spray with insecticide	
Leaves & fruit sticky. Black sooty mould	Whitefly or aphids	See pages 98 and 101	
Mottled leaf blades	Virus disease	See page 104	
Leaves have dark green veins with yellow area between	Magnesium deficiency	Spray leaves with Epsom salt solution with wetting agent	Spray twice each season as routine.
Brown area on stem near to soil	Foot rot	Spray with Benomyl (if infection slight, otherwise destroy)	Use sterilised compost & strict hygiene.
Grey mouldy patches on stems	Botrytis (grey mould)	cut out with sharp knife — treat with Benlate	Increase ventilation Remove old leaves. Do not overcrowd plants.
Flowers drop off at knuckle	Blossom drop	None	Spray flowers with water often. Tap them.
Fruit stops growing when match-head size	Dry set	None	Spray plants with water morning and night. Damp down well on hot days.
Bad area at bottom of the fruit (see page 92)	Blossom end rot	None	Correct watering, especially when plants are fruiting.
Fruit has small transparent ring with dark spot in centre	Ghost spot	None — affected fruit good to eat	Avoid splashing fruit, and as grey mould above.
Stalk end of fruit does not ripen	Green back	None	Shade and feed weekly. Do not remove the leavesfrom above unharvested trusses. Grow an immune variety.
Fruit are split. Sometimes mould grows in the split	Split fruit	None	Water regularly as splitting is caused by sudden growth after a dry period. Try growing a thicker skinned variety.

Making & Using Tomato Feed

1. Pour 5 litres (1 gal) of water into a plastic bucket.
2. Add 750g (1.5lb) of potassium nitrate and 180g (6oz) of ammonium nitrate.
3. Stir until the powders are dissolved.
4. Transfer to a plastic bottle, suitably labelled.

To use: add 5ml (1fl oz) of the solution to 5 litres (1 gal) of water and apply at every watering.

98 *(above) Tomato plants may also be grown in large pots in the greenhouse*

are carefully adhered to. Home-made tomato feed produces good results and is much cheaper than the liquid concentrates.

It is usual to feed tomato plants by watering the compost, plants can be foliar fed by watering the diluted feed directly onto the leaves. Never feed a very dry wilting plant, water it first and leave it to recover before feeding.

Four Methods of Growing Tomatoes

If tomatoes are grown in the same soil each year it is very likely that problems will occur with soil pests and soil borne diseases. Various methods of producing tomatoes have been devised and the ones described in the charts on pages 80-1 are all well tried and tested.

99 *Tomato plants growing in a straw bale*

Growing Tomatoes — Four Different Methods

1 • In a Soil Bed

1 As soon as the bed is free from its previous crop, dig into the soil a liberal quantity of *well-made* organic waste compost or *well-rotted* farmyard manure. Dig as deeply as possible without bringing any subsoil to the surface. The compost or manure should be well mixed with the soil and not, as is sometimes recommended, placed in the bottom of a trench.

2 Spread ground limestone over the surface at the rate of 300g per square metre (10 oz per sq yd).

3 Allow the bed to settle for at least two weeks (longer if possible).

4 Mark out the positions of the tomato plants. Allow a minimum of 40cm (16in) between the plants. If two rows are to be planted they should be 1 metre (1yd) apart.

5 Dig a hole, large enough to take the root ball. Tap the plant from its pot and place it in the hole. Firm the soil around the plant, taking care not to disturb the root ball.

6 Train and care for as described on pages 76-7.

7 When the first truss is set (ie the flowers have fallen and pea-sized fruit is present) begin feeding and continue to do so for the rest of the season.

2 • Growbags

Most manufacturers recommend three tomato plants per growbag. The author finds a better yield per bag, as well as less disease and water stress, if two plants are grown in each. Four pieces of wood nailed together into a tight surround for each bag is beneficial as it increases the bag's effective depth. (See Fig 39 page 35.)

1 Purchase *good quality* growbags.

2 Place the bags in their positions on the floor of the greenhouse. Drop a string for each plant from the glazing bar above. Tie each string around the bag, leaving a little slack to twist around the plant as it grows.

3 Cut three (or two) holes in the top of the bag, large enough to take each plant.

4 Carefully pour 10 litres (2 gal) of water into each bag.

5 Make appropriate sized holes in the growing medium by pushing the material sideways.

6 Tap the plants from their pots and place one in each hole. Draw the growing medium around the rootball.

7 Train and care for as described on pages 76-7.

8 Begin to feed as soon as the first fruit is set and continue throughout the season.

Hydroponics
This is growing plants without soil. Many commercial growers use a hydroponics system, called nutrient film technique (NFT) to produce tomatoes on a large scale. The roots lie unsupported in a black polythene channel and a nutrient solution is pumped continuously over them. This solution contains all the essential elements in the correct proportions and at the correct pH level.

Most systems are computer controlled and fully automatic. This technique removes the

3 • Ring Culture

1 Remove the soil from a soil bed (or use a wooden box), line with plastic and cut drainage holes.

2 Fill the hole (or box) with coarse sand, coal ashes or other non-toxic free draining material.

3 On the top of the sand place bottomless 22.5cm (9in) pots or whale hide rings 40 cm (16in) apart. Empty plastic containers, with tops and bottoms removed, may also be used.

4 Pot up the tomato plants into the bottomless pots using a good potting compost. Leave 2.5cm (1in) unfilled to make watering easier.

5 Water and care for as described but in addition to watering the pots, soak the material upon which they are standing.

6 After the first truss has set, feed the plants with liquid tomato fertiliser on the top of the compost only. Fertiliser watered on the sand will drain away and be wasted.

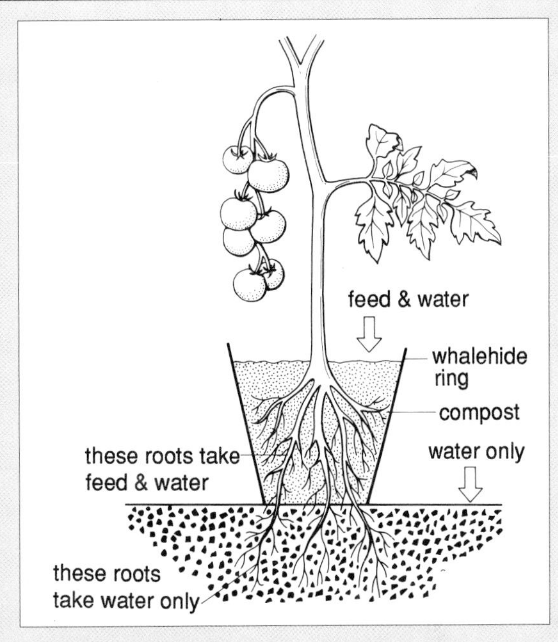

100 Ring culture

4 • Straw Bales

1 Three weeks or so before tomatoes are ready for planting, obtain a rectangular straw bale (wheat is best) and position it in the greenhouse. *Important:* check that the straw has not been treated with weed killer!

2 Soak the bale with water and pour 5 litres (1 gal) of water over it every other day. 'Feed' the bale with a high nitrogen fertiliser twice each week. (Gardens Direct market a fertiliser specially for this purpose.) Note that the bale may heat up, so take care not to plant up if it is too hot for the roots, ie over 30°C (85°F).

3 Make two holes in the bale with a sharp knife (not easy!) each large enough to take the tomato root ball.

4 Remove the pots from the tomato plants and place one in each hole.

5 Care for as described on pages 76-7.

6 Keep the bale watered and after the first truss is set, feed each week with tomato fertiliser.

need to feed and water, but all the other operations are carried out in a way similar to those described in this book.

The main advantage of hydroponics is that there are no soil-borne pests and diseases and the need to provide peat, or some other form of sterile growing medium, is removed.

Various hydroponics systems are available for amateur growers to use and these can be fun to try. The author finds that growing tomatoes by hydroponics to be either extremely successful or a complete disaster!

Cucumbers, Peppers, Aubergines & Melons

Cucumbers

Cucumbers can be satisfactorily grown in the same greenhouse as tomatoes — the common belief that this is not so should be ignored. A well-grown cucumber plant will produce up to fifty full-size cucumbers during the growing season.

The cucumber plant produces both male and female flowers. Unlike other species the cucumber produces a fruit from *unpollinated* flowers; fruit from *pollinated* flowers is bitter and not

101 Misting the cucumber plant with water from a sprayer takes only seconds and helps to control red spider mite. Later in the season the base of the stem was surrounded with a 22cm (9in) depth of compost, held in position with a plastic ring. A total of forty-six cucumbers were harvested from this single plant

very nice to eat. The aim of the greenhouse gardener is to produce fruit from unpollinated flowers, this can be achieved in two ways:

- By removing all the male flowers before they open.
- By growing a variety of cucumbers that has no male flowers — just female.

The second method is strongly recommended.

Cucumbers grow very quickly but they require a warmer environment than tomatoes, if the greenhouse is not heated it is essential that sowing is delayed until the cherry trees are in

102 A cucumber leaf with magnesium deficiency. Compare with the healthy leaves on the plant above

full blossom. Cucumber plants are easy to grow, but they are also easy to kill. The instructions in the chart should be followed carefully, with attention to detail.

Peppers

When well grown in an unheated greenhouse sweet peppers will produce a very worthwhile crop. Unlike cucumbers and tomatoes, peppers freeze well and a temporary glut is therefore not a problem. Green peppers, like green tomatoes, are unripe red or yellow ones. Larger crops will be obtained if the fruit is harvested whilst still green, as ripening takes a long time.

Pepper plants thrive in similar conditions to tomatoes so the two crops can be grown in the same greenhouse.

Aubergines

Aubergines are grown in the same way as peppers with some important exceptions:

- Seeds must be sown in January or early February as a longer growing season is needed.
- Somewhat cooler conditions are required in summer for the fruit to set; positioning near to a bottom ventilator will probably ensure setting.
- Aubergines must be harvested while the skins are still shiny. Fruit that has become dull is rather tough and unappetising.

Melons

The introduction of F1 varieties of melons (eg Sweetheart) has made their growing in a cold greenhouse well worthwhile. The fruits are much smaller than imported melons but the flavour is excellent. The best time to sow is when the cherry blossom is fully out, if a propagator is not available plants should be purchased one month later.

Growing Peppers

1. Sow seeds during March and germinate in a propagator set at 18°C (65°F).
2. Prick the seedlings out into 10cm (4in) pots of multipurpose compost and place on shelves or staging.
3. If frost is forecast, cover the plants at night with horticultural fleece.
4. When the roots are filling the pot transplant into either
   - a soil bed, 40cm (15in) apart
   - a growbag, three plants per bag
   - 22cm (9in) pots, one plant per pot.
5. Support each plant with a single cane and a string tie.
6. Keep a sharp lookout for aphids — see page 97-8.
7. Water regularly and feed each week with a liquid tomato fertiliser.
8. Harvest the fruit as soon as they are a reasonable size, by cutting through the stalk with a sharp knife.

103 A melon plant with two leading shoots, both being trained upwards

Growing Cucumbers

Raising the Plants

1 Select an F1 hybrid variety that produces only female flowers.

2 Use *clean* 15cm (6in) pots and *two-thirds* fill with a sterilised, free draining seed compost.

3 Hold one seed between finger and thumb and push it into the centre of the pot to a depth of 1cm (½in).

4 Water the pots and place them in a propagator set at 25°C (75°F) or the highest setting if it is lower than this.

5 After germination, which takes about three days, leave the plants in the propagator. Make sure that there is some ventilation and the propagator top is as clean as possible to admit maximum light.

6 When the seedling reaches the top of the pot, add extra compost up to within 1cm (½in) of the seed leaves.

7 Feed the plants each week with half-strength tomato fertiliser.

8 When daytime temperatures are above 21°C (70°F), remove the plants from the propagator and place them in the lightest part of the greenhouse. At night cover them with a piece of horticultural fleece.

Planting

1 Use a growbag, or a 30cm (12in) pot filled with a good *free-draining* potting compost, or a straw bale (treated as for tomatoes).

2 When the plants have enough roots to hold the root-ball intact (but before the roots circle the bottom of the pot) water well. Carefully knock each plant out of its pot and plant it with the minimum of root disturbance, leave the surface of the root-ball four or five centimetres (a couple of inches) higher than the compost. If a straw bale is used, sit the plant on top of the bale and pile compost around it.

3 Water well.

4 For the next few days, isolate the plants from the rest of the greenhouse with a sheet of polythene and maintain a humid atmosphere around them.

Training

Robinsons of Winchester plant support brackets are ideal as they are easily attached to any glazing bar.

1 Tie strings or wires across the area where cucumbers are to be grown. Horizontal wires should be 25cm (9in) apart.

2 Tie the main stem loosely and vertically to one of the supporting strings.

3 Remove all the sideshoots and flowers from the bottom 20 cm (8in) of the main stem.

4 As new sideshoots appear tie them along the horizontal strings.

5 When there is a sideshoot growing along each support, remove all other sideshoots as they appear, including sideshoots on sideshoots.

If a variety that produces male flowers is grown the training is a little different. With these varieties the fruits are produced on the sideshoots and not the leaf joints. Pinch the sideshoots off one leaf after each developing fruit.

Growing

1 Cucumbers use twice as much water as tomatoes so water regularly and do not allow the plants to dry out. Take care not to leave the plant stem in a pool of water or it will rot. Always damp down after watering to maintain a humid atmosphere.

2 Feed weekly with half-strength liquid tomato fertiliser.

3 Have a pressure sprayer permanently pumped-up and filled with clean water. Whenever you go into the greenhouse give the plants a quick misty spray, this will help to control red spider mites.

4 Add more compost and pile it around the stem base, a large plastic ring (section from a lemonade bottle) is a useful aid, especially for plants in growbags. This encourages extra root growth and increases production at the end of the season.

Harvesting

1 Do not delay harvesting as this will reduce the yield.

2 A cucumber is ready to harvest when its lower end is becoming rounded.

3 Hold the cucumber in one hand and cut through the fruit's stalk with the other.

4 Remove the harvested fruit from the greenhouse straightaway and wrap it in a single layer of clingfilm. Store cool.

Cucumber Trouble Shooter

Symptoms	*Cause*	*Treatment*	*Prevention*
Seedlings thin at base and topple over	Damping off	None at this stage	Use sterile compost. Spray with Cheshunt
Rotting fruit, mouldy patches on stems	Grey mould	Spray with Benlate	Avoid over-watering
Soft brown rot at base of stem	Basal stem rot	Dust with sulphur Pile compost over infected area	Keep base of stem dry
White powder on leaf surface	Powdery mildew	Spray with Benlate	Keep soil moist at all times. Ventilate well
Pale spots on leaves which grow and turn brown	Leaf blotch	Remove and burn infected leaves. Dust with sulphur	Use sterile compost. Ventilate well
Spots on fruit which ooze amber gum	Gummosis	Remove & destroy infected fruit. Spray with Dithane	Reduce humidity. Grow a resistant variety

Growing Melons

1 Sow seeds individually in 9cm (3.5in) pots filled with a multipurpose compost, by holding in between the finger and thumb and pushing them one centimetre (half an inch) deep.

2 Germinate in a propagator at 21°C (70°F) and grow the young plants in good light on the staging or a shelf.

3 When the plants are large enough, transplant into a soil bed which has been well manured with rotted farm yard manure or well-made organic waste compost. (Growbags or 23cm (9in) pots may be used instead.)

4 Arrange strings, a net or trellis on which to train the plants.

5 Water regularly, but avoid getting the soil too wet.

6 Tie the leading shoots upwards (there is often more than one). When they are about 1 metre (1yd) long, pinch out the tops.

7 Train side shoots either horizontally or in a fan.

8 A female flower should be produced on each sideshoot. One leaf beyond this flower, pinch out the growing point.

9 Make sure that there is a good tie either side of the female flower, this will support the fruit and there will be no need for a net.

10 During bright sunshine remove a fully open male flower, take off its petals and transfer pollen to the female by touching the flower centres together.

11 Remove a second male flower, take off its petals, place it inside the female flower and leave it there.

12 Pollinate several flowers at the same time, but do not attempt to grow more than six fruits per plant or they will be very small.

13 When the fruits begin to change colour, reduce watering and give plenty of ventilation. This is necessary as a fungus control measure.

14 Test for ripeness by taking the fruit in your hand and applying a little gentle pressure to the blossom end. If the fruit gives a little it is ready for harvest.

15 Cut through the stalk with a sharp knife and keep the melon in a warm room to complete ripening.

16 When all the fruit has been gathered, remove the plants and place on the compost heap.

104 Male and female melon flowers. The hoverfly — a friend of the gardener — is on the male flower

Strawberries

Strawberries can be produced at least four weeks earlier in a cold greenhouse than outside. As strawberry plants age they lose their vigour, it is essential therefore to obtain plants, either by propagating from a young healthy bed or by purchasing certified plants in the autumn. The variety Gorella is probably best for a cold greenhouse but any early variety can be used.

Growing Early Strawberries

1. In early July fill 15cm (6in) pots with potting compost and partially sink them alongside the best plants in a strawberry bed. Peg one runner into each pot and nip off the stem to prevent any more runners from forming.
2. When the runners have rooted, detach them from the parent plants *or* pot up purchased plants.
3. Plunge the pots into a bed of soil, sand or coal ashes. During August and September keep the plants growing with a weekly feed of liquid fertiliser.
4. Leave the plants outside until January, this is very important as a period of cold is essential for bud formation.
5. In mid-January, take the plants into the greenhouse and either arrange them on the staging, or transplant them into a growbag (six plants per bag).
6. Water as required — but not too much!
7. When the first flower buds can be seen, begin a weekly feeding routine with a low-strength liquid fertiliser (Chempak Formula 4 or similar).
8. As the weather becomes warmer, increase daytime ventilation.
9. Brush the open flowers with cotton wool or a rabbit's tail. The flowers are self-fertile but the pollen has to move from the male to the female parts.
10. Pick the fruit as it ripens.
11. After fruiting, discard the plants as they will not force successfully the following year.

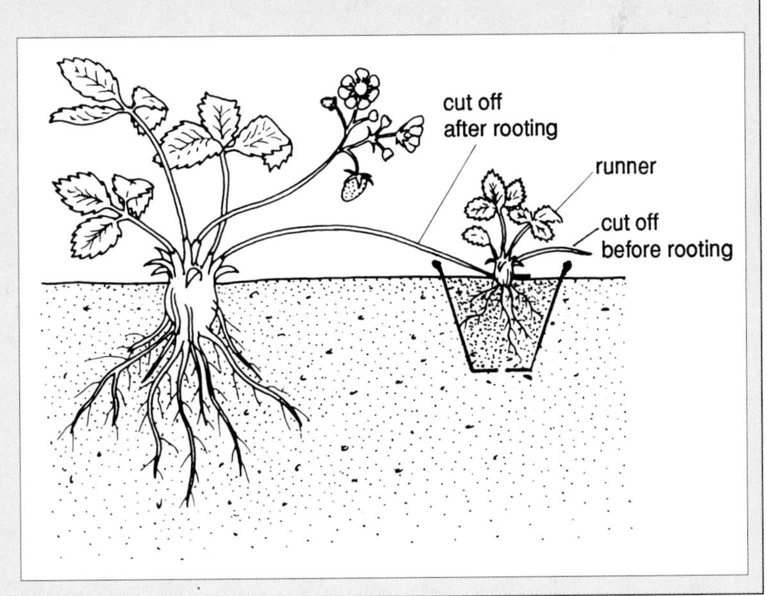

105 Propagating strawberry plants

Growing Grapes in Small Greenhouse

1 Mark out an area of slightly more than 1 metre (1yd) square, either inside or just outside the greenhouse.

2 Dig out the soil to a depth of at least 60cm (2ft), pile up the topsoil and discard any subsoil that is brought to the surface.

3 Place a layer of brick rubble in the bottom and cover this with a layer of inverted turfs.

4 To the pile of topsoil add:

five 10 litre (2 gal) buckets of well-made organic compost or well-rotted farmyard manure.

300g (0.5lb) of ground limestone

100g (3oz) bone meal

a spadeful of woodash if available.

5 Mix the topsoil and return it to the hole.

6 Obtain a container-grown vine of a variety which is suitable for a cold greenhouse. (Black Hamburg or Fosters Seedling [white] are suitable but new ones are being developed which may be better.)

7 Dig a hole larger, but not deeper, than the container.

8 Remove the container, tease out the roots and spread them in the bottom of the hole. Fill in the hole, making sure that the vine is not planted any deeper than it was in the container.

9 Tread to firm the soil and water well.

10 If planted outside make a hole through the side of the greenhouse to thread through the main stem of the vine. Fill the gap around the stem with sacking.

11 If the vine is dormant, cut back to one metre (1yd) after planting. If the vine is a young growing one cut right back, leaving just two buds, as these develop, train the better one as a leader and cut the other one off.

Grapes

A grape vine grows very rapidly and may fill a small greenhouse during its first season. Controlling rank summer growth and thinning bunches of grapes is very time consuming, if time is short this crop is best left to others.

The method described allows grape production in a small greenhouse. Grapes can be grown in pots or boxes; the principle is exactly as outlined in the growing instructions, but watering and feeding are more critical.

An alternative method of training is illustrated on page 90. Here a four-year-old vine which had previously grown across the roof was cut down to a rod just 1 metre (1yd) long. A vertical net was erected and the strongest shoots which grew were threaded through this to give complete cover. Once the shoots reached the outside of the frame they were stopped. Throughout the rest of the season any new shoots that appeared were nipped off.

This method took less space and less time than previous years when the rod extended along the roof and training was more orthodox.

This method does not give bunches of grapes hanging from the greenhouse roof, but it gives a good yield and other plants have more light.

12 Decide where the vine is to grow and fix wires accordingly. If the main stem is to be taken along the roof it should be on the north side to restrict the shading on other plants.

13 As the leader grows tie it along the wire.

14 Laterals (side growths) will appear, these should either be trained at right angles to the main stem or removed.

15 Nip off all the non-fruiting laterals after the seventh leaf.. Nip out the tips of the fruiting laterals, leaving two leaves between the fruit and the end.

16 Water regularly, vines need large amounts of water and must not be allowed to dry out.

17 After flowering give a liquid feed each week with half-strength tomato fertiliser.

18 Aim for one bunch of grapes per 20cm (8in) of stem. Cut out all the other bunches.

19 When the grapes are about the size of small peas, thin out the individual bunches. Use a pair of fine pointed scissors (special grape scissors are available) and, working from the bottom, snip out small clusters of grapes leaving individual grapes with about 1cm (½in) between them. Failure to do this results in useless tiny fruit and a lot of fungus disease.

20 Throughout the summer the vine will produce more sideshoots and flowers. Rub these out as they arise.

21 Harvest the grapes as they ripen by cutting off whole bunches with secateurs.

22 Reduce watering.

23 When the plant is dormant cut back the main rod (stem) to leave about one metre (one yard). Any laterals that remain on this should be cut back to two buds.

24 Rub the old wood hard with a gloved hand to remove loose bark.

25 Remove all dead leaves and prunings.

26 When growth begins the following spring, sprinkle 100g (3 oz) of complete fertiliser around the base and apply a thick mulch to the soil.

When to Sow Vegetables in a Cold Greenhouse

Vegetable	*Sowing Time in the Greenhouse*
Half-hardy vegetables, eg runner beans, French beans, sweetcorn, courgettes	4-6 weeks before the last date that frost is possible
Broad beans	February
Carrots	February, also early variety in July if space allows
Brassicas	4 weeks before planting out time. Although hardy they still need hardening off. Avoid checks to growth, especially with cauliflowers
Celery & celariac	mid-February to mid-March
Parsley	February and again in early August

106 A vine being trained in the greenhouse on a vertical net. The black plastic sheeting on the floor prevents weed growth and helps to retain moisture

107 The same vine three weeks later. Once the net is covered all new shoots are pinched out as they appear. This vine produced fourteen large bunches, mostly near the bottom of the plant

Vegetables

Earlier and better vegetables are produced from plants that arte raised in the greenhouse. In addition a few can be grown to maturity before the greenhouse becomes crowded with flowers and fruit.

Beans

Broad beans grown as described on page 92 will crop in June and be free from blackfly. A temporary glut is not a problem as they freeze extremely well.

A large crop of French beans is also obtained by this method. French beans are subject to red spider — keep a sharp lookout and refer to Chapter 6.

When correctly placed, runner beans can make a feature in a flower garden — attractive and also productive.

Brassicas

Brussels sprouts, summer and winter cabbage, Kohl rabi and cauliflowers can all be grown in this way. Crops raised by this method produce much better and more reliable yields than bare rooted transplants grown outside.

For a very early crop of cabbage in a cold greenhouse, sow Hispi (or Kingspi) seeds in February, germinate in a propagator and plant out into a greenhouse bed. Hearted cabbage will be ready well before tomato planting time.

Carrots

Carrots and parsnips are vegetables that should not be transplanted, but, if space allows, a very early and a very large crop of carrots can be grown in a greenhouse soil bed. There is the additional advantage that there is no carrot fly!

108 Just for fun! Carrots grown to maturity in a root trainer. Carrots do not normally transplant

109 (right) Sweetcorn plants ready for hardening off. The root trainer has been opened up to show how the root system develops

Celery & Celariac
Celariac is an excellent and very hardy vegetable — it is also much easier to grow than celery.

These crops will bolt if they receive a check during the early stages of growth. A check is caused by a sudden drop in temperature, or the plants becoming root bound.

Onions & Leeks
Grow in the same way as described for celery. Some growers prefer to sow these seeds very thinly and transfer them outside directly from the seed tray, if this method is practised sow three or four weeks later.

Marrows, Courgettes, Pumpkins & Squashes
These take up much space and are therefore unsuitable for growing to maturity in an amateur's greenhouse. Good crops can be obtained outside from plants raised in the greenhouse.

Mint
Fresh mint can be available all winter by the simple method described in the chart on page 93.

Parsley
This herb is easily grown from seed and with the use of a greenhouse, it can be available throughout the year. Parsley is a biennial and will go to seed in its second year, so raise new plants each spring and discard the old.

Peas
Peas are fairly hardy and an early crop can be obtained by sowing an *early variety* in February in a greenhouse bed. Alternatively the method

Using the Greenhouse to Grow Vegetables

Broad Beans

1 Select a green seeded variety and sow each seed individually in a 9cm (3.5in) pot filled with multipurpose compost. (*Large* root trainers are better and take less space.)

2 Germinate in a propagator with a low setting 13°C (55°F).

3 As soon as the seeds have germinated, transfer them to the staging.

4 Water regularly, but do not allow them to become waterlogged.

5 In extremely cold weather cover with fleece, broad beans are frost hardy but they will be damaged if the compost freezes (see page 13).

6 When the plants are about 15 cm (6in) tall, harden them off and plant outside.

French Beans

1 Prepare a greenhouse soil bed with plenty of well-rotted farmyard manure (or substitute).

2 Select a *climbing variety* of French bean.

3 Six weeks before normal outdoor sowing time, raise the plants as described for runner beans.

4 Push the longest possible canes into the soil bed, 45cm (18in) apart in a square, or 30cm (12in) apart in a line.

5 Plant one bean by each cane and twist the top into a climbing position.

6 Keep well watered and give the flowers a fine spray on sunny days.

7 Pick the beans regularly as soon as they are big enough.

Runner Beans

1 Select a stringless variety.

2 **One month before** the time these crops are normally sown outside, sow seeds individually in 9cm (3.5in) pots filled with a multipurpose compost. (Large root trainers or peat pots are better.)

3 Leave on the bench to germinate.

4 Water regularly — but not too much.

5 As soon as the danger of late frost has passed, harden them off and plant outside.

Brassicas

1 Sow seeds in a tray of seed compost.

2 Germinate on the greenhouse staging, or in a propagator at 15°C (60°F).

3 As soon as the seedlings are large enough to handle, prick them out into root trainers or individual pots filled with potting compost.

4 Grow on until the compost is filled with roots.

5 Harden off and plant outside.

Carrots

1 Prepare a soil bed by adding *well-rotted* farmyard manure or substitute. (The common belief that this will cause roots to fork is probably untrue.)

2 Rake the surface to produce a fine, level and even tilth.

3 Select an early variety of carrot (not Rondo, as they are too small).

4 In late January or early February, sprinkle seeds *thinly and evenly* over the bed.

5 Rake lightly to cover the seeds.

6 Water well, using a fine rose.

7 Pick out any weed seedlings as they germinate. This takes only a few minutes each week and once the carrots have grown, new weeds will not have enough light to compete.

8 When the roots are large enough harvest as required.

Celery & Celariac

1 Late February or early March sow seeds in a shallow pot filled with seed compost.

2 Germinate in a propagator set at 18°C (65°F).

3 Prick out into individual pots 7cm (3in) or similar sized sections in a tray, filled with a good potting compost.

4 Place on the staging, water as necessary and give a little feed after four weeks.

5 Harden off with care as soon as the roots have filled the pot and plant outside.

Fresh Mint in Winter

1 In September, dig up some mint rhizomes (underground stems) from outside plants.

2 Three-quarters fill a 22cm (9in) pot with potting compost.

3 Place six or seven 10cm (4in) lengths of rhizome (each with at least one bud) on top of the compost.

4 Fill the pot with compost and water well.

5 Leave the pot on the staging and do not allow it to dry out.

6 Fresh shoots will soon appear and can be used as required.

Marrows, Courgettes, Pumpkins & Squashes

1 Six weeks or so before the last frost is likely, sow seeds individually in 13cm (5in) pots, filled with multipurpose compost, by holding each between the finger and thumb and pushing it into the compost.

2 Germinate on the bench or in a propagator 18°C (68°F).

3 Grow on until the danger of frost is passed.

4 Harden off and plant outside.

Using the Greenhouse to Grow Vegetables

Parsley All-Year Round

1 In early spring fill a six-section tray with seed compost.
2 Place two parsley seeds in the centre of each and sprinkle a *little* compost over them.
3 Water with a rose can.
4 Leave uncovered on the staging and water as necessary.
5 When the plants are about 5cm (2in) tall remove them complete with an undisturbed root ball and plant them in either a greenhouse soil bed 15cm (6in) apart, or individually in 12cm (5in) pots filled with a good potting compost.
6 Give a light feed every two weeks.
7 Harvest as required by taking the largest leaves complete with stems. Never take more than half the leaves from an individual plant.

Sweetcorn

1 Fill a block of large root trainers with seed compost.
2 Sow when the cherry trees are in full blossom.
3 Push one seed into each section to a depth of 5cm (2in).
4 Water well and place on the staging.
5 Three or four weeks after germination give a light feed with a high nitrogen fertiliser.
6 As soon as the risks of frost are over, harden off and plant outside.

Peas

1 In February cover an outside area with clear plastic to warm the soil.
2 Obtain 1 metre (1yd) lengths of plastic guttering.
3 Fill to within 2cm (1in) of the top with soilless compost.
4 Place an early variety of pea seeds on the compost surface about 7cm (3in) apart in an irregular pattern.
5 Fill to the top with compost.
6 Water and leave on the greenhouse staging to germinate and grow.
7 When the weather is suitable, remove the plastic and make gutter-size trenches in the soil.
8 Place the peas in the trenches and slide out the gutter.
9 Cover with fleece, to protect from cold winds and birds.

described starts the seedlings in the greenhouse, before tranferring outside.

Sweet Corn

Varieties are now available that produce good cobs outdoors in most areas of Britain.

When planting out, arrange the plants in a square as this will aid complete pollination.

Although sweetcorn plants can be grown in individual pots, the method described here is better as it takes up less space and produces a better root system.

6

Pests, Diseases & Their Control

Many of the problems described in this chapter will not be encountered if good hygiene and husbandry are practised. This is summarised in the ten points listed below:

- Carefully inspect any new plant for adult pests, larvae and eggs before putting it into the greenhouse.
- Store pots, trays and composts in a shed and not the greenhouse.
- Control weeds both inside and outside the greenhouse.
- Remove plant debris and unwanted plants from the greenhouse immediately.
- 'Spring' clean each autumn. Empty the greenhouse and thoroughly wash all glass, staging and equipment — put a little garden disinfectant into the water.
- Always used sterilised compost for seeds and seedlings.
- Put used compost on the compost heap, or use it outside as a mulch. Never use it for a second time.
- Water and feed regularly.
- Give plants plenty of room and move pot plants apart as they grow.
- Remember that a well grown vigorous plant is much less likely to suffer from pests and disease than one which is badly grown and overcrowded.

Greenhouse Pests

Hundreds of different species of insects, spiders and other creatures enter a greenhouse during the course of a year. Of these 99 per cent will do no harm at all, in fact some do good by pollinating flowers and eating pests. Some of the plant feeders may multiply to the point where they cause damage to greenhouse plants. These species are called pests. In order for a species to become a pest it must have the following:

- an abundant food source
- the correct environment
- freedom from predators (creatures that eat them)
- freedom from parasites
- freedom from disease

If a chemical that kills all creatures is sprayed into a greenhouse, any new pest that enters will increase in number very quickly as all its predators and parasites will have gone. In practice no available spray will kill everything, as the occasional pest or egg will always survive. Better control is achieved when pesticides are only used as a last resort, and the chosen pesticide is one which kills only the target pest leaving its predators and parasites unharmed.

Weak, sickly or overcrowded plants are much more likely to have infestations of pests than the healthy and well-spaced ones. A clean, tidy and well-organised greenhouse will harbour fewer pests than an untidy one with rubbish piled under the staging.

Pests can be introduced with purchased and

free gift plants. Any new plant should be checked for pests and quarantined for a few days before being taken into the greenhouse.

Chemical Control

All pesticides must be used with extreme care and the health hazard warnings heeded!

Chemicals which have been approved for pest control are sold under different names by different manufacturers; BioSprayday, Fumite, Murphy whitefly smoke, Picket and Nippon all contain permethrin as the active ingredient — they are of course different in other ways — the method of application for example.

Note that the word 'pesticide' means a substance that kills pests, while an 'insecticide' kills insects, a 'fungicide' kills fungus, etc.

The various methods of applying chemicals to pests are:

- as a dust, the powder floats around the plants and some settles on the pests.
- as a liquid spray, tiny particles of water carry the pesticide.
- as an aerosol — a convenient form of liquid spray, with very fine droplets.
- as a 'systemic' preparation. The chemical enters the plants' tissues and sap. When the plant is bitten, or the sap is sucked, the creature gets some poison as well.
- as a smoke. In the evening the greenhouse is sealed, the gardener lights the touch paper and withdraws. The pesticide is carried in a dense smoke that fills the greenhouse, by morning the smoke will be gone and most of the pests will be dead. This method is also known as fumigation.

110 A smoke cone

Do not spray:

- in cold damp weather or when the greenhouse cannot be ventilated — fungus disease could result.
- in bright sunshine or the leaves may be scorched
- when bees are working
- if biological control creatures have been introduced.

Biological Control

Biological control is the introduction of a creature that will eat or parasitise a certain pest. A 'do it yourself' method of biological control would be to collect ladybirds and release them into the greenhouse to eat aphids.

Using Biological Control

1. In early summer when the pest is present and weather conditions are fairly warm, purchase the correct biological control creature (suppliers are listed in the reference section).
2. If the control organism is a flying insect, remove any sticky yellow traps.
3. Introduce the control organisms according to the instructions that arrive with them — this is easy but important.
4. Continue to ventilate but try not to allow the greenhouse to become too cold.
5. Water and feed the plants as usual but on no account do any spraying that could harm insects. (A systemic fungicide could be used but check that it does not contain an insecticide.)
6. Look out for signs that the introduction has been successful — with whitefly, black scales (instead of white) will be seen after ten days or so.
7. Do not expect instant control.

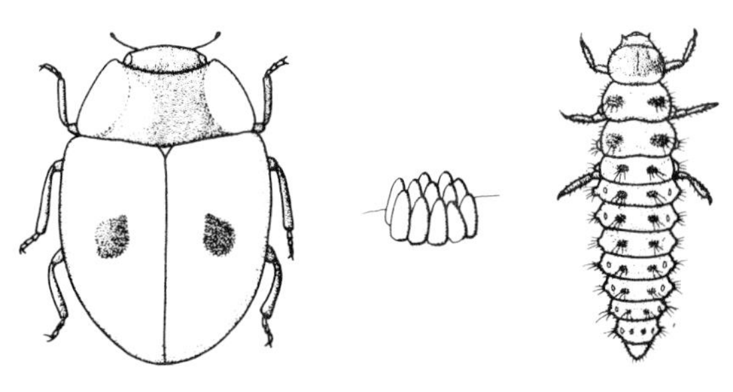

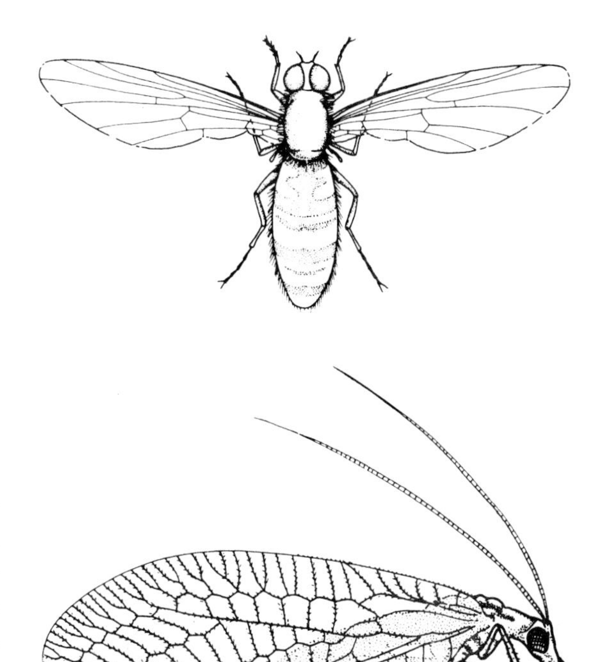

110, 111, 112 Natural biological control of aphids. Ladybird (above, shown as adult, egg and lava), hoverfly (top right) and lacewing (lower right) all reduce the aphid population

The creatures which are purchased for biological control are specially bred predators and parasites of greenhouse pests. Biological control creatures are used to keep the pest numbers low and prevent them from causing damage. A well-grown plant will not be harmed by the few pests needed to provide food for the purchased creatures.

Aphids in the Greenhouse

Early Detection

1 Some plants are more likely to be infested than others, be extra vigilant with Impatiens (Busy Lizzi) and peppers.

2 Look for small white 'insects' on the upper surfaces of leaves (these are often mistaken for whitefly but are in fact the aphids' skins which have been shed as they grow).

3 Take special note of the growing tips of plants and the underside of upper leaves.

4 Ants are easily seen, as they move fairly quickly. If you see any on your plants it is a sign that aphids are present as well.

Control

1 If there is just an occasional small colony — squash it between finger and thumb.

2 If just a few pot plants are infested, tip each upside-down and immerse it in a bowl of soapy water for a few seconds. Lay the plant on its side and direct a jet of water to wash off the wetted aphids.

3 If the weather is not too cold, move infected plants outside, cooler conditions and natural predators will often reduce aphid numbers and the plants may recover.

4 If these methods do not work, spray with 'Rapid' this quickly kills aphids and does not harm some of the aphids' predators.

5 As a last resort, fumigate the house with a smoke cone.

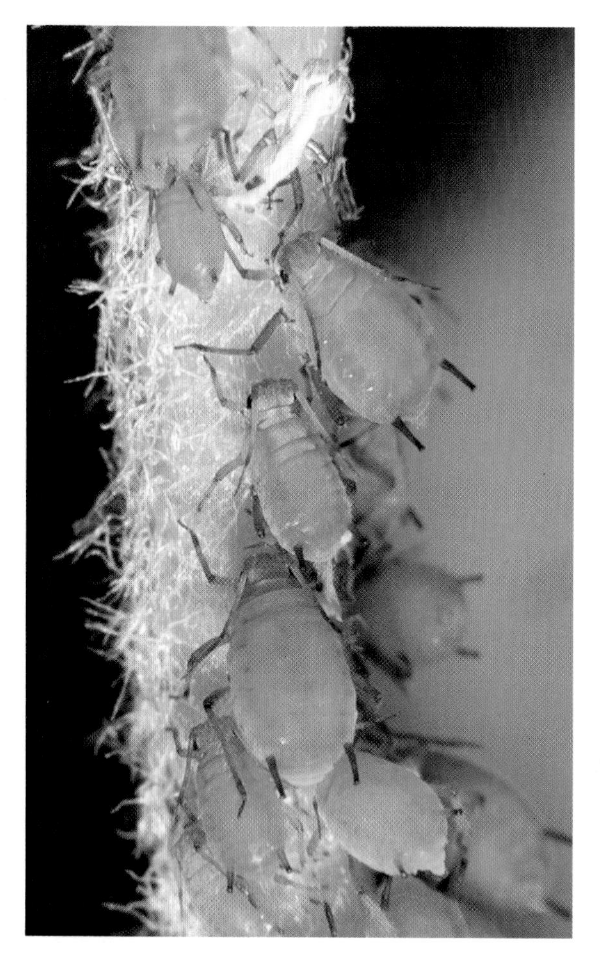

114 *(left)* *An aphid colony*

115 *(below)* *Larva of hoverfly feeding on aphids*

For many years commercial cucumber growers have relied entirely on biological control to prevent whitefly and red spider from causing damage. These growers actually introduce some pests to keep good populations of control organisms. The greenhouse gardener will not have to do that!

Biological control is not cheap nor easy, but it is very effective when correctly carried out.

Aphids

'Blight', 'greenfly' and 'blackfly' are common names given to hundreds of different species of plant-sucking insects called aphids. The size, shape and feeding method are the same for all aphids and so is the damage they do to plants.

Aphids damage plants in four ways:

- They suck sugar from plant vessels (veins); this robs the plant of the energy and material for growth.
- They distort plant growth, making young leaves curl as they grow.
- They drop unwanted sugar (honeydew) on the plant making it sticky. Sometimes a black sooty mould grows in this, making the plant unsightly and depriving it of light.
- They spread virus diseases from one plant to another.

All the aphids on greenhouse plants are female and they lay babies at an alarming rate. It is this rapid build-up of numbers that makes the aphid such a difficult pest. As with all pests, early detection is an important part of control.

Note that organic growers would not use methods 4 and 5 in the chart. If average tem-

116 Leafminer damage

117 The light-coloured spots on this leaf were made by red spider mites. A sharp lookout should be kept for this first sign of infection, especially during hot weather. At this stage control measures are likely to work and little damage will have been done

peratures are above 15°C (60°F) the biological control mites (*Aphidoletes*) can be purchased. The orange larvae of these mites feed on aphids, and when fully grown they fall to the ground to pupate.

In addition to the well-known aphid predators like ladybirds, hoverfly and lacewing larvae, aphids are subject to fungus diseases and parasites. Sometimes you will see fairly large bronze aphids standing motionless on the underside of leaves. These are quite dead and the parasite that killed them will be around and hopefully laying its eggs in more aphids.

Eelworm

Eelworms are microscopic worms that live in the soil. There are hundreds of different species and only a few do harm. The one which sometimes causes trouble in the greenhouse is the root-knot eelworm. This forms swellings on the roots of many plants including begonias, chrysanthemums, cucumbers, tomatoes and lettuce. Eelworms are spread through infected soil or compost.

Signs of damage by root-knot eelworm:

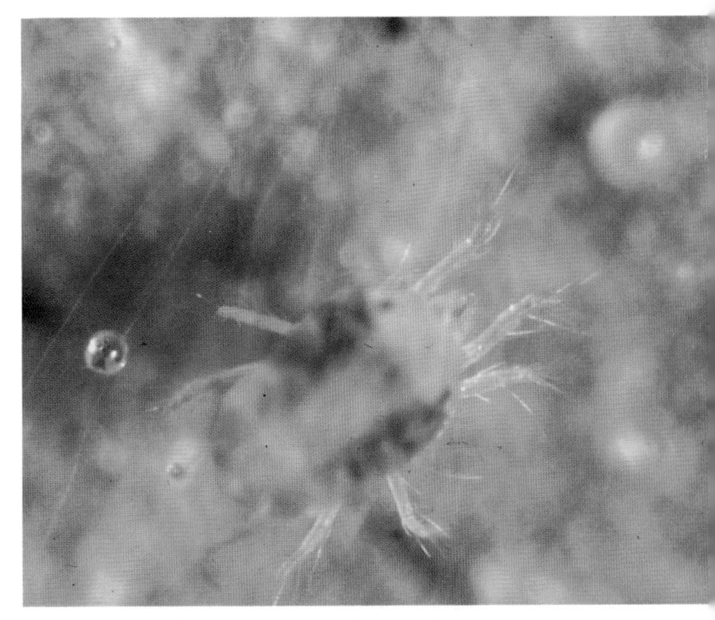

118 A magnified photograph of red spider mite and eggs on the underside of a leaf. They are not red, and the actual length of a fully grown mite is less than 1mm

Controlling Greenhouse Pests

Root Knot Eelworm

1 Do not introduce suspect plants into the greenhouse.
2 Destroy infected plants *and* the compost they are growing in.
3 If infection occurs, change the staging gravel and/or capillary matting.
4 Change the soil in infected beds.
5 Maintain strict hygiene with tools, pots, etc.
6 Use growbags or straw bales instead of a soil bed.

Leafminers

1 Inspect any new plants which are taken into the greenhouse.
2 Pick off any infected leaves while the larvae or pupae are still present and destroy them.

Red Spider Mite

1 Learn to recognise the mites — use a hand lens.
2 As soon as yellow specks are seen on the upper surface of leaves, examine the underside for mites. (Yellow spots are not always caused by mites.)
3 Control weeds and rubbish both inside and around the outside of the greenhouse.
4 Be very thorough when cleaning out the greenhouse in autumn, use a garden disinfectant.
5 Take extreme care not to introduce mites with new plants.
6 Spray susceptible plants with clean water as often as possible. Mites thrive in hot, dry conditions but not in cooler, humid conditions.
7 Spray with Fumite or Vitax aerosol.
8 If mites are present (especially in early summer, as a temperature of 18°C [65°F] is necessary), purchase the biological control organism (*Phytoseiulus*). This organism is also a mite, it feeds on red spiders and will give good control throughout the summer.

Whitefly

1 Check any new plants before taking them into the greenhouse. Use a hand lens and look underneath the leaves for eggs and larvae (called 'scales').
2 Control weeds both inside and outside the greenhouse.
3 Spray or fumigate with an insecticide and repeat every ten days (eggs and scales are resistant to most sprays).
4 Introduce the biological control organism (*Encarsia*). This is a tiny parasitic wasp and providing the temperature is not too low, is very successful. If the introduction is successful, some of the whitefly scales will become black.

Vine Weevil

1 Remove any debris which could harbour adult weevils.
2 Knock out any suddenly wilting plant and examine the compost for larvae.
3 Drench the compost with BioHexyl.
4 Purchase the biological control organism.
5 Use John Innes compost instead of a non-soil compost.

- plants wilt easily
- stunted growth
- 'under nourished' appearance, ie pale foliage
- roots have irregular swellings on them that prevent the uptake of water and nutrients.

Leafminers

A leafminer is a small fly that lays its eggs in a leaf. The grub that hatches from an egg feeds inside the leaf, leaving a snake-like track that gets wider as the grub grows. After a while the grub turns into a pupa, these can be seen as bumps at the head of the 'snake'. Several plants are subject to leafminers but chrysanthemums are most often affected.

Leafminers damage plants in the following ways:

- leaves are made to look unsightly.
- small white spots on the foliage caused by adults feeding.

Red Spider Mite

Red spider mites are extremely serious greenhouse pests. Mites are very difficult to see on a leaf without the aid of a magnifying glass, but are more easily seen on their fine webs as they travel from one leaf to another. Mites hibernate in and around the greenhouse throughout the winter in large numbers; an infection one year almost guarantees problems the following year.

Mites feed by sucking sap from the leaves, this causes tiny yellow spotting on the upper surface. As infestation increases the leaf turns yellow, hard and covered with fine cobwebs.

Red spider mites are resistant to many chemical sprays and this makes their control very difficult.

Red spider mites damage plants in the following ways:

- weaken the plant by removing sap
- yellow spots on the upper leaf surfaces
- plant becomes covered with webs, cutting off light and preventing air movement
- older leaves turn yellow and brittle
- the plant often dies.

Whitefly

A common pest of greenhouse plants is a small white fly only 2mm (1/16 inch) long, it spends most of its time underneath the leaves but flies off when disturbed. Its larvae are also white and they can be seen as scales on the underside of the leaf. Both adults and larvae feed by sucking sap from the plant.

The skins that fall from aphids are sometimes mistaken for whiteflies, the fact that the adults take off when disturbed is a good way to recognise this pest.

Whiteflies damage plants in the following ways:

- weaken them by removing sap
- make them sticky with honeydew
- make them black, as a sooty mould grows in the honeydew.

Note that the greenhouse whitefly is a different organism to the one that is sometimes seen on brassica plants.

Vine Weevil

These small brown, wingless beetles hide during the day and feed on plant leaves at night. They lay their eggs in the compost, which hatch into creamy white larvae. The larvae feed on plant roots and cause very serious damage. Pot plants such as fuchsias, cyclamen, African violets, and begonias are very susceptible to vine weevils.

Vine weevils damage plants in the following ways:

- eats holes in leaves, this is much less serious than the root damage
- eats roots, this causes sudden wilting and often death.

The biological control organism for vine weevil is very successful. It is a microscopic worm which enters the larvae, kills it with a bacterium and then feeds on it. The worm requires a temperature of 14°C (58F) and can only work when weevil grubs are present. The preparation which contains the worms is called Biosafe, or is available by post from Defenders Ltd (called NemasysH).

119 (left) Glasshouse whitefly and their eggs on a tomato leaf

120 (below) Vine weevil larva

Fungus Diseases

Fungi are an essential part of the living world, they break down humus and produce plant nutrients in the soil. A few species of fungus feed on living plants — these cause disease.

These diseases are invisible until the fungus begins to reproduce and turn areas of the plants mouldy. The moulds produce millions of minute spores that float in the air. Fungus spores act like plant seeds — they germinate and spread the species. Fungus spores only germinate in humid conditions, this gives gardeners their first line of defence, for if the greenhouse has plenty of air and is not too humid, diseases are much less likely to appear. The second line of defence is to use sterilised composts.

Damping Off

Circular patches of seedlings sometimes 'neck' at the base and fall over, on close inspection a discoloration can be seen and later a mould

121 Typical fungus on the underside of a leaf. The body of the fungus is deep inside the leaf and is feeding on the living plant. The parts seen are the fruiting bodies which will be producing millions of spores — the fungus equivalent of seeds

122 Cress seedlings grown in sterilised and unsterilised soil. The pot on the right is infected with the fungus disease called 'damping off'. In the pot on the left the spores which cause this disease have been killed off by sterilisation (see pages 30-1)

123 Grey mould on a cyclamen

appears. This is 'damping-off' fungus and it is most likely to happen in damp, cold and overcrowded conditions. Lettuce, antirrhinums, lobelia and petunias are very susceptible to this disease.

Damping off can be controlled by sound greenhouse practice, which is better than spraying with fungicides.

Downy Mildew

This disease is most often seen in winter lettuce but it affects a very wide range of plants, particularly in autumn when temperatures drop and humidity increases. Pale angular areas appear on the upper leaf surface and on the underside is a mould.

Grey Mould

This is a very common disease that affects a lot of different plants. It is easily recognised by the fluffy grey mould which sometimes 'smokes' as spores rise in millions. It is most often seen on bedding plants, chrysanthemum flowers, cucumber fruits, lettuce, tomato stems, strawberries and vines.

Powdery Mildew

This disease is most often seen on the leaves of chrysanthemums, cucumbers, pot plants, strawberries and vine. Parts of the plants, especially the leaves become covered with a white powder. Unlike the other fungus diseases this one occurs in hot and dry conditions. Overcrowded

Controlling Greenhouse Diseases

Damping Off of Seedlings

1 Use clean seed trays.
2 Use sterile compost for seed sowing.
3 Sow seeds evenly and *thinly.*
4 Use clean tap water for seedlings.
5 Do not get the compost too wet.
6 If using a propagator maintain some ventilation.
7 Keep the temperature high enough for rapid germination.
8 Destroy infected compost.
9 If all else fails, water with Cheshunt compound.

Downy Mildew

1 Pick off infected leaves.
2 Ventilate well.
3 Avoid overcrowding.
4 Water the soil and not the leaves.
5 Resistant varieties are being developed, consult the seed catalogues and try one.

Wilts

1 Practice strict greenhouse hygiene.
2 Sterilise canes and boxes which have been in contact with infected plants.
3 Wait for the soil to warm up before planting out.
4 Spray Benlate on the stem bases immediately after planting out in greenhouse beds.

Grey Mould

1 Pick off the infected parts and remove them.
2 Avoid overcrowding.
3 Do not allow plants to wilt.
4 Ventilate well to prevent a humid atmosphere.
5 Spray with a systemic fungicide.
6 Some plants have been bred with resistance — use them.

Powdery Mildew

1 Do not overcrowd plants.
2 Provide adequate ventilation.
3 Spray with a fungicide.
4 Organic growers may spray with bicarbonate soda solution (5g per litre with soft soap as a wetting agent).
5 Use growbags instead of soil beds.
6 Grow resistant varieties.

Virus Diseases

1 Strict hygiene — wash hands after smoking and before touching tomatoes.
2 Control sucking insects as they spread the diseases from plant to plant.
3 Take cuttings from healthy plants and never from plants which may be diseased.
4 Wherever possible use varieties that are resistant to virus diseases.

plants are more susceptible than well-spaced ones. The spores overwinter on dead plant tissue; a thorough autumn clean is essential in the control of this disease.

Wilts

The lower leaves of some plants wilt, turn yellow and shrivel. If the stem is cut a few centimetres above soil level a brown stain can be seen. The disease progresses up the plant, which may die if the infection is severe. This condition is caused by one of the wilt fungi.

Commonly affected plants are begonias, chrysanthemums, courgettes, cucumbers, and fuchsias. If this disease is present in soil beds it will persist for several years.

Virus Diseases

There are many virus diseases, some cause mottled leaves or streaked flowers while others

Trouble Shooter — Pests and Diseases

Problem	*Possible Solution* *Chemical Methods*	*Organic Gardening Methods*
seedlings damping off	Cheshunt compound	good hygiene, use sterilised compost
other fungus diseases: downy mildew grey mould powdery mildew	BioSupercarb TumbleBlight (not for edibles) pbiDithane Benlate	good hygiene grow only resistant varieties control powdery mildew with bicarbonate of soda (5g per litre) with soft soap as wetting agent(powdery mildew only)
general insect pests	Fumite Sybol Vitax aerosol BioCropsaver Vitax areosol Tumblebug	Phostrogen Natural Organic Derris dust insecticide soap insecticides containing pyrethrum only
ants	Doff Nippon ICI Ant Killer Dust	pour boiling water into nests
aphids	Rapid (harmless to most useful insects)	insecticidal soap biological control — *Aphidoletes*
caterpillars	Picket	hand picking biological control — *Bactospeine*
earwigs	Picket	trap in an inverted pot filled with straw
mealy bugs	Fumite	remove with meths on an artist's brush biological control — *Cryptolaemus*
red spider mite	Fumite Vitax aerosol	maintain cool humid conditions biological control — *Phytoseiulus*
scale insects	any systemic insecticide	wipe off with cotton wool soaked in meths
sicarid flies (fungus gnats)	drench compost with insecticide	repot in fresh compost — use JI compost biological control — as for vine weevil
slugs	ICI slug pellets Murphy Slugit	hand picking at night with torch traps of half beer half water + a little sugar*
whitefly	Murphy whitefly smoke Fumite smoke cone	Yellow sticky traps; suck up with a vacuum cleaner biological control — *Encarsia*
woodlice	ICI wasp killer dust Doff	remove hiding places kill with boilingwater
vine weevil	drench soil with BioHexyl	biological control — *Steinernema* sold as NemasysH and Biosafe

* A nematode which kills slugs is being researched, but at the time of writing it had not been released. It may be available now — check with Defenders Ltd.

Identifying Plant Diseases

Symptons Observed	*Disease*
Seedlings falling over in wet patches — a mould may, or may not be seen	Damping off
Pale green patches on upper surface with a white mould underneath. Usually in cool conditions.	Downy Mildew
A fluffy grey mould which make 'smoke' when touched	Grey mould
Leaves covered with a white powder	Powdery Mildew
Lower leaves wilt and turn yellow. This condition progresses up the plant	Wilts
Leaves develop a mosiac of dark and light green	Virus diseases
Tomato seedlings do not grow and turn purple (Take care! Do not confuse with the blue caused by cold)	Virus diseases

cause stunted or distorted growth. Virus diseases can only avoided, they cannot be cured.

Virus diseases are spread from one plant to another by sucking insects and tiny worms (nematodes) which feed on roots. Some virus diseases are spread through the seeds.

Some common virus diseases are:

- ***Cucumber Mosaic*** — Yellow patterns on the leaves of cucumbers and courgettes
- ***Tomato Aspermy*** — Plants become bushy with mottled leaves and small fruit.
- ***Tomato Mosaic*** — Seedlings turn purple; older plants have mottled light and dark green patches with some distortion. Leaf blades may not form, brown patches under the surface of green fruit — a very infectious disease.

124 Not all virus 'diseases' are harmful, the decorative patterns on some house plants, like Abutilon and this Piggy-back plant, are caused by a virus

Glossary

alpines	small plants from mountain districts. Usually very hardy but damaged by high winter humidity.
annual plant	a plant that grows from seed, flowers and dies in one growing season.
auxin	a chemical substance, present in plants, which controls growth.
balanced fertiliser	a fertiliser which contains nitrogen, phosphorus and potassium in the required proportions.
bedding plant	a plant grown to provide colour in a flower bed for only one season.
biennial plant	a plant which grows from seed, flowers the following year and then dies.
biological control	a method of controlling pests by the introduction of an organism.
bolt	begin to flower before making normal vegetative growth.
brassica	a member of the cabbage family.
break	buds beginning to grow lower down the stem.
calyx	the outermost part of a flower still attached to the fruit.
capillary bed	a greenhouse bed which lifts water to its surface.
capillary matting	a material with fine pores which soaks up water.
carbon dioxide	a gas which forms 0.04 per cent of air. This is absorbed by plant leaves and part is used to make plant tissues.
compost	a material which is used in plant pots and trays instead of soil.
cropped headed bolt	a bolt with a head shaped to lock into a slot. This eliminates the need to drill a hole.
cutting	a part removed from a plant, which will produce roots and form a new plant if given the right conditions.
damping down	wetting the greenhouse floor.
Dexion	(trade name) angled steel or aluminium alloy strip with holes and slots, used for fabrication.
ecosystem	a natural area with all its plants and animals.
ericaceous	acid (the term used for composts suitable for growing heathers etc).
F1 hybrid	the first cross between pure bred parents.

fertiliser	a substance which contains chemicals necessary for plant growth.
fleece	a non-woven fabric which transmits light; used to protect plants.
fungus	a large group of organisms which feed on organic matter while growing inside it. The fruiting bodies of a fungus grow outside its food at a very fast rate.
harden off	gradually acclimatise a greenhouse plant to outside conditions.
humidity	the dampness of the atmosphere.
intercropping	growing a crop between the rows of another.
jardinières	decorative containers to conceal plant pots.
John Innes Compost	a compost made from soil, sand and peat to a recipe developed by the John Innes Institute.
kilowatt	an amount of electricity (1,000 watts).
lateral roots	roots which grow sidewards from the main vertical one.
legume	a member of the pea and bean family.
loam	soil formed by stacking turf and leaving it to decay.
macro-nutrient	a chemical which plants require in 'large' amounts.
micro-nutrient	a chemical which plants require in very small amounts.
mite	a very small eight legged creature (an insect has six legs).
multipurpose compost	a compost which may be used for sowing seeds, striking cuttings and potting up.
nitrogen	an element essential for plant growth, it is a gas and forms almost 80 per cent of the air. When combined with other elements it forms a salt. Plants can only absorb nitrogen as a salt, they cannot take it from the air.
node	the place on the stem where the leaf joins. There is almost always a bud at a node.
parasite	an organism which feeds on or in a single animal or plant.
peat	partially decayed plant material, hundreds of years old.
perennial plant	a plant which lives and flowers for several years.
Perlite	rock which is heated to very high temperatures, it expands and forms a light, inert material which can be used in various composts.
pH	the units by which the degree of acidity is measured.
phosphorus (phosphate)	a chemical element which is essential for plant growth.
plunge bed	a thick layer of sand or peat into which potted plants are sunk to the level of the top of the pot.
pollination	the transfer of pollen to the female parts of the flower.
potassium (potash)	a chemical element which is essential for plant growth.
potting up	transferring a seedling, or small plant to a plant pot.
potting on	transferring a plant from a small pot to a larger one.

predator	an animal which eats other animals.
prick out	transferring seedlings to pots or trays.
propagation	raising new plants.
propagator	an enclosed space for raising new plants, it has a transparent top and may have a heated floor.
residual current device	a safety feature in an electric circuit which cuts off the current if a fault arises.
rooting powder (or gel)	an auxin (plant hormone) which reduces the time cuttings take to root.
runner	a long horizontal stem which has plantlets along its length.
side shoot	a shoot which arises in a leaf joint of the main stem.
solenoid valve	a device for turning water on and off which is operated by an electric current.
spore	a very small 'seed' produced by a fungus.
stool	the roots and ground level parts of a plant.
stopping	pinching out the growing point of a plant.
systemic insecticide	a chemical substance which is absorbed by plants and makes the sap poisonous to insects.
thermostat	a device which turns heating on or off when a certain temperature is reached.
trace element	a chemical substance which is essential to plants in very small amounts.
truss	a cluster of tomatoes attached to one point of the plant's stem.
tuber	a swollen root or underground stem.
variegated leaf	a leaf with two shades or colours.
vegetative	growth other than flower or fruit.
Vermiculite	a rock which is heated to high temperatures to expand it. The resulting crumbs are very light and used in horticulture for composts.
virus	an extremely small organism which can only 'live' in living things. It causes diseases in plants and animals.
water stress	reduction in plant growth caused by too little water.
watt	the basic unit of electricity.

Reference Section

Greenhouse Accessories
The following items are suitable for **all** greenhouses and are available from:

Robinsons of Winchester Ltd
Chilcomb Lane
Chilcomb
Winchester
Hampshire
SO21 1HU
☎ 0962 844755

Benching — two tier
Blinds — roof, internal and external
Brackets — for crop support wires
Heaters — electric fan, thermostatically controlled
Nuts, bolts and fittings — aluminium
Potting tidy
Propagators — electric
Roof vent openers — automatic
Shelving — slatted
Staging — slatted
Thermometers — max/min
Vents — side, six-bladed louvre
Watering kit

Mist Propagating Equipment & Automatic Watering Systems

Access Garden Products
Crick
Northampton
NN6 7XS
☎ 0788 822301

Electronic & Technical Services Ltd
Unit 32
The Price Street Business Centre
Price Street
Birkenhead
Merseyside
☎ 051 670 1897

Simply Controls
139 The Commercial Centre
Picket Piece
Andover
Hampshire
SP11 6RU
☎ 0264 334805

Thermoforce Ltd
Camplex Plantcare Division
Heybridge Works
Maldon
Essex CM9 7NW
☎ 0621 858797

Low Voltage Propagators

Elemental Systems Ltd
Park Royal Industrial Estate
12 Gorst Road
London NW10 6LE
☎ 081 961 3466

Soil Warming Cables & Soil Sterilisers

Thermoforce Ltd
(see above)

Warrick Warming Cables
101 Sedlescombe Road North
St Leonards
East Sussex
☎ 0424 446310

Biological Pest Control Organisms

These are obtainable through some garden centres and seed firms (eg Marshalls and Chase Organics). Specialist suppliers by post:

Defenders Ltd
PO Box 131
Wye
Ashford
Kent
TN25 5TQ
☎ 0233 813121

Bunting & Sons
The Nurseries
Great Horkesley
Colchester
Essex
CM6 4AY
☎ 0206 271300

English Woodlands Ltd
Hoyle Depot
Graffham
Petworth
West Sussex
GU28 0LR
☎ 07986 574

Natural Pest Control
Watermead
Yapton Road
Barnham
Bognor Regis
West Sussex
PO22 0BQ
☎ 0243 553250

Fertilisers & Specialist Chemicals

Garden Direct
Geddings Road
Hoddesdon
Herts
EN11 0LR
☎ 0992 441888

Vitax Ltd
Owen Street
Coalville
Leics
☎ 0530 510060

Propane Gas Heaters

Aeromatic-Barter Ltd
Kynoch Road
Eley's Estate
Edmonton
London N18 3BH
☎ 081 803 8302

Paraffin Heaters

George H. Elt Ltd
Eltex Works
Bromyard Road
Worcester
WR2 5DN
☎ 0905 422377

Hotbox Heaters Ltd
Mill Lane
Lymington
Hants
SO4 9A2
☎ 0590 683788

Horticultural Fleece

Agralan
The Old Brickyard
Ahston Keynes
Swindon
SN6 6QR
☎ 0285 860015

Major Seed Companies

Samuel Dobie & Son
PO Box 90
Paignton
Devon TQ3 1XY
☎ 0803 616281

J. W. Boyce
67 Station Road
Soham
Ely
Cambs CB7 5ED
☎ 0638 721158

D. T. Brown & Co Ltd
Station Road
Poulton-le-Fylde
Blackpool
FY6 7HX
☎ 0253 882371

Mr Fothergill's Seeds
Gazeley Road
Kentford
Newmarket
Suffolk CB8 7QB
☎ 0638 751887

S. E. Marshall & Co
Regal Road
Wisbech
Cambs PE13 2RF
☎ 0945 583407

Suttons Seeds Ltd
Hele Road
Torquay
Devon TQ2 7QJ
☎ 0803 612011

Thompson & Morgan
London Road
Ipswich
IP2 0BA
☎ 0473 688821

Unwins Seeds
Histon
Cambridge
CB4 4LE
☎ 0945 588522

Chase Organics (GB) Ltd
Addlestone
Surry
KT15 1HY
☎ 0932 820958
(This firm supplies seeds and organic gardening items on behalf of the Henry Doubleday Research Association who run the Centre for Organic Gardening at Ryton near Coventry.)

Kings Crown
Monks Farm
Pantlings Lane
Coggeshall Road
Kelvedon
Essex CO5 9PG
☎ 0376 570000

Reference Books

The Plant Finder
Lists over 60,000 plants, from alpines to trees and where to obtain them. The lay gardener's 'bible', updated annually. A comprehensive section on plant names.

The Vegetable Finder
Compiled by the Henry Doubleday Research Association. Lists sources for all commercially available vegetable varieties.

Both published by MPC

Index